BE YE RECONCILED

THE ENEMY'S GREATEST FEAR

A journey to experiencing
healing in *all*
your relationships—
*so far as it **depends on you**.*

TIM CAMERON

BEST-SELLING AUTHOR OF
THE FORTY-DAY WORD FAST

Published by Insight International, Inc.
contact@freshword.com
www.freshword.com
918-493-1718

ISBN: 978-1-960452-13-9
E-Book ISBN: 978-1-960452-14-6

Library of Congress Control Number: 2025906164

Printed in the United States of America.

Contents

FOREWORD

Dear One,

It is not often that a book brings me to tears, nor is it often that a book instigates true change in my perspective. *"Be Ye Reconciled"* is such a book—it has done both in my life.

I love to read, but often I am a disinterested observer in what I read rather than an active participant. Let me explain. I have found that often I am able to read a well-written book with little to no emotional attachment on my part and without feeling a need to change. I can read these wonderful books while staying in a safe place of self-imposed mediocrity and average contentment.

While *"Be Ye Reconciled"* is certainly well-written and its message is wonderful, it is more than that. So much more. This is a dangerous book. It is not soft, nor is it winsome, but it holds a gravitational force of undeniable power.

So I guess what I want to tell you is this: Do not read this book.

Do not read this book unless you are desperate for change in your heart and in your relationships.

Do not read this book unless you believe obedience to Scripture is of utmost importance.

Do not read this book unless you want to spend time on your knees.

Do not read this book unless you long for forgiveness to flow from you to others.

Tim Cameron is a dear friend of many years, and I have watched his life intently. I have regarded Tim as he walked through physical pain with his eyes and heart set on Jesus. I have listened as he navigated difficult conversations with wisdom and compassion. I have been a front-row observer to a life of immaculate moral integrity and a heart that burns with a passion to know God and to be used of Him.

Tim's writing shouts of truth and rings of eternal wisdom. His perspective on reconciliation, forgiveness, and repentance has been birthed in an intense study of the Scriptures. Although *"Be Ye Reconciled"* is theologically sound, make no mistake about it; this is not a dry, academic discourse on the importance of reconciliation. *"Be Ye Reconciled"* is an invitation of the very best kind—an invitation to live a life of unmatched joy and heartfelt purpose.

So now I dare you.

I dare you to read *"Be Ye Reconciled"* with an open heart and your hands raised in worship.

I dare you to read this book with a desire to be changed.

I dare you to read this book humbly yet with great anticipation.

I dare you to be changed into His likeness as you give your heart and your relationships to the One who made you.

It seems fitting to close this foreword with a prayer not of my own writing but of a man, like Tim, who knew the value of surrender.

We thank You, O Lord, holy Father, Almighty, everlasting God, who has satisfied the hunger and thirst of our souls with the spiritual food of the body and the blood of Your Son Jesus Christ our Lord; and we beseech You, O merciful Lord, that this sacrament may be the washing away of our iniquities, the strength of our weakness, and our defense against the dangers of the world. O Lord, let this communion cleanse us from sin and prepare us to be partakers of heavenly joys; through Jesus Christ our Lord. Amen.

—BISHOP OF SALISBURY (nineteenth century)

Carol McLeod
Author, Speaker, Podcaster

ACKNOWLEDGMENTS

I want to honor my remarkable wife, Annamae. She has been my best friend for over fifty years. What a treasure! And my delightful family.

And then there are my superb, lifelong friends. You know who you are. You have stood with me, held me up in the wilderness, and stuck closer than a brother.

Carolyn Bass, my editor, thank you for the excellent support.

INTRODUCTION

Everything in our soul aches for the marriage of heaven and earth—that forecast place where we find the sweet waters. Heaven, flush with contentment, peace, and the very presence of God. It is the destination that Reepicheep speaks of in C. S. Lewis' *The Chronicles of Narnia*. A poem propelled him in his quest for the Far East. It said,

Where sky and water meet,
Where the waves grow sweet,
Doubt not Reepicheep,
To find all you seek.
There is the utter East.[1]

Heaven is a place where there will be no division. All who name Jesus as their Lord will be like liquid gold—broken families united, severed friendships restored, tepid acquaintances embraced, and enemies forgiven. Oh, the glory, to fall on our faces and join the twenty-four elders and cry out with the living creatures, "Holy, holy, is the Lord God Almighty" (Rev. 4:8-11). We, weeping, rejoicing, dancing, worshipping at the sight of our beautiful Savior, Christ Jesus. Ignite your imagination; see Noah, John the Baptist, Teresa of Avila, Mother Teresa, and the many saints. One by one, I want to meet the ten martyrs whose statues stand above the West Door of Westminster Abbey, London. What were these martyrs' lives like, those who dared to stare down death?

Can you envision a place where the sweetest springs of God's kindness envelop you? A place where you receive the inheritance of peace? It will not be like any peace you have ever experienced or imagined. Stop right now and read this carefully and slowly. God's design makes this heavenly comfort come to your life in the present tense. The kingdom of God yearns to come to life in your midst. God desires for heaven to touch the earth where you live. Yet it hinges on this ineffable experience, unity with God and others. Ponder deeply in your soul this consideration, that experiencing heaven this very moment and at the end of your life too rests in the daring decision to pursue peace with all men and women.

Satan's all-encompassing goal is to wipe out unity wherever it exists. His goal is utter destruction and propagating the lie that unity isn't the great necessity. He revels in his deviousness, luring believers from the gospel's truth. The fact is that Christ wants the sweet sound of harmony to come into our relationships. *Unity* is God's *essential purpose*.

Our Lord is interceding for us from heaven. He prays that schisms in His body are healed and that the power of the Holy Spirit will overcome the rifts in all relationships. Oh, that we would humble ourselves and give the Lamb the reward of His suffering—oneness in His body. He prays that we would love Him so profoundly we would lay down our offenses, grievances, hurts, bitterness, and unforgiveness. Unity is Christ's highest and most all-encompassing prayer (John 17).

We too are propelled into that quest where sky and waters meet, the thin space[2] where heaven and earth touch. There we are reconciled to Christ and the members of His body. Can you hear the invitation of the Holy Spirit as He whispers? He calls you by name to leave familiar, safe, religious surroundings. The Spirit beckons you to enter strange lands and waters from which no return can be unscathed. You cannot ignore it. The quest strikes at your very core. Once you begin, you must let no obstacle stand in your way. It will be one of the most significant undertakings of your life.

You will butt against mountains; ford dangerous, troubling waters; and perhaps encounter demons. Your heart will be broken. Pride will take a direct hit.

For those who take up this journey, their outward appearance will also change. Others will notice the difference. You will bear the marks of our Savior. And if they can persevere through the most significant challenges, even the aroma of their lives will change. When others look at them, the features of their faces will look familiar to the One we all long to see, Christ.

You will be inwardly transformed for the rest of your life. Through the power of the Holy Spirit, you will return victorious, with humility borne from the work of forgiveness and reconciliation.

Saint Patrick, the fifth-century apostle of Ireland, wrote of this transformation that only Christ can perform in his historic prayer, "Saint Patrick's Breastplate."[3]

Christ with me,
Christ before me,
Christ behind me,
Christ in me,
Christ beneath me,
Christ above me,
Christ on my right,
Christ on my left,
Christ when I lie down,
Christ when I sit down,
Christ when I arise,
Christ in the heart of every man who thinks of me,
Christ in the mouth of everyone who speaks of me,

Christ in every eye that sees me,
Christ in every ear that hears me.

This transformation will make a man or woman settle for nothing less than peace and unity in life and relationships. This thought is scandalous considering our culture of conflict and division in the world and churches.

Dare we take up the quest of reconciliation? To serve Him as He deserves? To fight and not heed the wounds? We must have all of Him; we must say yes.

As I pen these words, demons tremble;
Satan's schemes are exposed and brought to light.
And he, the grotesque angel, with his angels, are put to flight;
the kingdom of this ruler begins to crumble.

CHAPTER 1

MY CONFESSION

I heard much talk about those *other* churches growing up—disparaging remarks about the Methodists, unflattering comments about Catholics, and the error of the Church of Christ. And those Assemblies of God and Pentecostals, well, they were just too different (strange). And what about those Mennonites I went to school with? What was that about? Christianity seemed like a fractured mess.

And me? I thought I was a Christian but struggled mightily with the basics of Christianity: unforgiveness, jealousy, lust, and lying. It seemed like I got resaved at least once a month. It made no difference—an organ or an out-of-tune piano, a stellar soloist or a novice song leader—all it took was another chorus of "Just as I Am," and I was up from my seat and at the altar. Did you sit on those pews the same way? Do you still sit on them?

But a feeling of salvation never seemed to stick. There were too many "don't do this and don't do thats." Invariably, those were the very things I did. I felt like the little kid playing Whac-A-Mole; as soon as I whacked a sin, another popped up, sometimes two.

My upbringing set the stage for a life of judging others, fault-finding, and a negative disposition. During my youth, one pivotal experience solidified this point of view—the little denominational church. And that incident I could never shake.

Daddy was a master of everything he could lay his hands on: leatherwork, plumbing, electricity, woodwork, sheetrock, and design. He was every small church's dream member. Dad was all in—tithing, devoting untold hours and resources to building, remodeling, and repairing anything at the beck and call of the pastor. Dad taught himself the piano to be the backup hymn leader—he really did—and, of course, taught Sunday school. Dad ensured the whole family was enrolled in those early morning classes before the main service. The gospel truth is that I had a perfect attendance pin for seven years of Sunday morning, Sunday night, and Wednesday night services. Whew!

I learned two things at church: I needed to be perfect, and I needed to perform. Those heavy burdens produced a ball and chain I dragged into my adult life and marriage. That cursed perfectionism and performance mentality bled into every facet of my life. But worst of all, I became *religious*—the appearance of godliness but denying its power (2 Tim. 3:5).

My grandparents had a radically different story from my parents'. As I reflect on my grandparents now—being a grandparent myself—I realize what marvelous people they were to me. They filled in all the gaps. I spent weekends, summers, and so many more days on their sprawling ranch with hundreds of acres, colossal hay barns, farm equipment, herds of cattle, a fifteen-acre pond, and many riding horses. Their land even had a bunkhouse with ranch hands. Grandma was the one who loaded my brother, first cousin, and me up every summer and took us across the country from the Great Salt Lake to Disneyland. However, my grandparents were functional alcoholics; there was never a dull moment with them. Grandma Ruby found a marriage with Grandpa Milford that finally stuck—it was her third.

Oh, how my parents loved their tiny country denominational church. The pastor was a loving and strong man. Grandma was a regular in that church, but Milford rarely graced the church door. He would show up periodically for a Christmas or Easter service. After many years at the church, my daddy, grandma, and the pastor zeroed in on Grandpa and coaxed him into giving the church a try. Amazingly, it stuck on Milford, and he became an official member. And Grandpa had a personal encounter with Jesus. Wouldn't you know it, he began applying his similar skill set to the church as Daddy. He constructed, by hand, the most beautiful pastor's podium for the church. It was a magnificent piece, made with multiple kinds of native wood, carvings, and luxurious features like a lock and key drawer for the pastor to keep an extra copy of his Sunday sermon, breath mints, and so on. Grandpa worked on it for months. Shortly after, he proudly gave the podium to the church, and it happened. The event changed his life for the rest of his life.

The church split began with some silly conflict over remodeling the sanctuary. Ultimately, the pastor quit. And we eventually left and found another church. Grandpa shook the dust off his feet and didn't grace another church building for years. He refused to return to religion except for an occasional Christmas service every few years. The enemy planted that perverse thought in my mind, and I believed it: My church was just like those *other* churches. Unity in the church? Ha! It didn't exist.

The stage was set for me. I longed—strived—for authentic community. But I never came wholeheartedly to Christ. I now know we can only come to others through Jesus. There is One who is our Mediator; He is the only way to fellowship with others. I had pipe dreams of community and went to outlandish lengths to pursue it. Yes, Annamae and I did sell everything, and I resigned from a fantastic job at a Christian university and joined a Christian commune—a first-class disaster ensued. I had a vision of community, and I would live it out. In reality, I was proud and self-righteous. My prescriptions of fellowship became judgments on others who couldn't measure up. Oh, as if I could!

I learned that Christian fellowship and community were always just a little beyond my reach, and no church experience with others lasted. Unity was not a divine reality for me. I believed this false narrative, and its fruit was a negative outlook that had destructive effects on my marriage.

I followed Jesus as best I could for decades, always cast in leadership positions in the church and at work. And then, in an instant, my world came to a grinding halt after a life-altering and career-ending medical event. Pain vanquished me. I shriveled up in chronic pain, and my gold-electro-plated spirituality melted. My mirage of self-sufficiency evaporated.

It is so embarrassing to think about those calls to my friends every week. I would be weeping in pain, desperate for someone to pray for me. I wanted to die. The years of chronic pain were too much. There were not enough drugs to ease the suffering.

Pain will shatter all illusions of religiousness. Unyielding pain will strip you naked—nothing will stand between you and God.

I was naked.

Over time, God allowed me to glimpse part of what He saw in me—a fearful, religious boy posing as a mature Christian man, a fraud.

My testimony now is that the years of pain and suffering pale compared to their majestic, transforming effects. I write this with a conscience clear of any rotting, smelly self-righteousness. God got ahold of me, and I grabbed on for life. I eventually submitted my will to His will the best I could, clouded vision cleared and ears opened. I discovered joy in Christ through the agony of pain and the marvelous fruit it produces in my life. The sisters from *God Calling* were spot-on: "Suffering borne with Me, must in time bring joy, as does all real contact with Me."[1]

I received a fresh revelation of God Himself. I crossed my ford to Peniel, where Jacob wrestled the angel, saw God face to face, and limped on his thigh (Gen. 32:22-32). I limp now too—three total knee replacements and back surgeries later.

The following prayer means so much to me. It epitomizes my journey with God—author unknown, attributed to a battle-weary Confederate Army soldier near the 'war's end.

"Confederate Soldier's Prayer"

I asked God for strength, that I might achieve;
I was made weak, that I might learn humbly to obey.
I asked for health, that I might do greater things;
I was given infirmity, that I might do better things.
I asked for riches, that I might be happy;
I was given poverty, that I might be wise.
I asked for power, that I might have the praise of men;
I was given weakness, that I might feel the need of God.
I asked for all things, that I might enjoy life;
I was given life, that I might enjoy all things.
I got nothing that I asked for, but everything I hoped for.
Almost despite myself, my unspoken prayers were answered.
I am among all men most richly blessed.[2]

And my marriage? As I write, I am in my fifty-third year and celebrating the most enriching of those. Listening to my wife is a joy and privilege integral to my life in Christ. Praying with her is glorious.

One stark revelation came from my years of physical suffering: I had been trapped in worldly systems of endless religious activity. Most of my fellowship with other Christians was paper-thin. As my intimacy with Christ deepened, the Holy Spirit prompted me to take stock of my relationships.

I began praying, "Holy Spirit, reveal to me anyone I have offended, anyone I need to ask forgiveness for, any debts I need to pay, or anyone 'I'm separated from." I forewarn you; it is a dangerous prayer—not a safe place for self. Honestly, I had no conception of the torrent about to be unleashed. The blindfold was stripped away, and the scales were scraped off my eyes. How could I not have seen it? A reservoir of broken relationships. Many were my fault; many were not. Some were the result of abysmal decisions; others came from gossip about the boss, and then those family disputes were out of my control. I discovered that these differences didn't make a difference—I lived separated from many other believers. I had unforgiveness in my life. I was unforgiven by others.

Thus began my quest to be united with God and reconciled to others through the power of the Holy Spirit and repentance. Along the way, I am discovering the exhilaration of forgiving and being forgiven. Be ye reconciled. This is the pursuit.

Be Ye Reconciled—the Enemy's Greatest Fear

We Christians are traditionally long on information and short on experiencing transformation. We have sprawling leadership conferences, popular podcasts, Christian bookstores, and churches on literally every block (of course, different denominations that seldom intersect). But we live in a day when being a Christ-follower makes you suspect to many people. I attribute this statement not to the stranglehold of the enemy's lasso on our Christian culture but rather to the failure of Christians to simply love one another.

A Pew Research Center report shows that the Christian majority has been shrinking for a long time, and if it continues Christians will fall to less than half of the US population in just years. However, I contend that what is just as alarming are the belief systems and doctrines of the millennials and Generation Z. If this offends you, I apologize; however, many

Christians in these groups hold dubious beliefs about the Bible's inerrancy or values held by followers of Jesus for quincentenaries.

The subtle, ever-so-unnoticeable move to live with unforgiveness and embrace division as just part of the normal Christian life has engulfed us. It dilutes, perverts, and hinders the message of the cross. This is not the normal Christian life! It is the worst example we can put forth as Christ's followers. It is not the gospel. It is a lie.

The third question of *17 Questions about Salvation, An Anglican Catechism*, states: How does sin affect you? Sin alienates me from God, my neighbor, God's good creation, and myself. Apart from Christ, I am hopeless, guilty, lost, helpless, and walking in the way of death (**Gen. 3:14–19; Ps. 38; Isa. 53:6; 59:1–2; Rom. 6:20–23**).[3]

Offense and division rule in the Christian church and its expressions: Protestants, Catholics, and all others. The distinguishing feature of Jesus' followers is not just what they teach but how they show their love for one another and live their lives.

Everyone has a profoundly moving story. But what about your story? Do you have the strength of character and relationship with Jesus Christ to fight this demonic trend of living with unforgiveness in relationships? My closest friends are praying with me that this little book will lead to an experience that will alter your life.

If any of these descriptions apply to where you are in your Christian experience, I implore you to read on.

If:

- You have broken relationships.
- You are willing to inquire of the Holy Spirit about the station of your relationships.
- You are confident everything is fine—it is all good.

CHAPTER 2

THE GREATEST MIRACLE

Heaven rejoices when "good" Christians, so sure of their righteousness, repent of their hard hearts. When we kneel at the foot of the cross, freely admitting to Him, and then to others, "I was wrong—I'm sorry," reconciliation spreads in waves.[1]

—M. BASILEA SCHLINK

What a mind-blowing, other-worldly thought: to be one with another person. Brace yourself and get ready to be jettisoned beyond your mind's comprehension. For not just one or a few but *all* of Christ's followers shall become one with the Father and the Son (John 17, Jesus' High Priestly prayer). Unity is the pattern that Christ has established in the heavens and is interceding for right now from His throne next to God the Father Almighty, maker of all things.

Hearken back to the very night before Jesus was crucified. He prayed these three things to the Father for the disciples: 1) that they would be cared for because they are in the world, 2) that they would be sanctified (purified and consecrated), and 3) that they would be one with each other in the same manner that the Father and Son are one (John 17:11, 17, 21, 23). It gives me chills to contemplate the reality of those prayers and the effect their fruition would have on our broken world!

However, for Christ's High Priestly prayer to be fulfilled in each one of us, there exists one glaring prerequisite we cannot skim over and must confront: that we would live a life of daily repentance and intimacy with the Holy Spirit. Without the Holy Spirit, we are powerless to evoke the love of Christ that breaks the yoke of pride that always stands guard as Satan's sentinel.

So here's the question: Do you experience signs, visions, or God's miraculous power through the Holy Spirit?

Many of us have seen this power at some point in our Christian life. Once you have experienced it, everything else the world offers is a pale imitation. Without the power of the Holy Spirit, you are left with religion—hollow, bland, and powerless talk. How tragic. It is sad because so many Christians have settled for religion. But even a miraculous encounter with the Holy Spirit a few years back or once a few decades ago is not God's intention. Without God's miraculous power in us daily, we are powerless against the enemy's plan to destroy our peace with others. Without God's might, we are like little stick figures, waving our arms and throwing pebbles at an advancing, demonic army. The operation of the Holy Spirit at work in our lives is our only hope.

Write down in the space below two times when you remember the power of the Holy Spirit at work in your life.

1. _____

_____

2. _____

_____

Now Let's Talk Miracles

Stick with me as we work our way to the greatest miracle of all.

The apostle John chronicled the miracles of Jesus in his Gospel—miracles with a capital M—inexplicable, staggering events the likes of which had never been witnessed before in his time. And John also noted that Jesus did *many* other signs before His disciples, not just a few more, but many. "Jesus performed many other signs in the presence of his disciples, which are not recorded in this book. But these are written that you may believe that Jesus is the Messiah, the Son of God and that by believing you may have life in his name" (John 20:30-31). What different kinds of miracles did He perform? What if He did miracles that have never been seen on earth before, thought about, or dreamed of? Oh my!

The original language is helpful in these verses (John 20:30-31) to reveal what John was trying to express when he recounted Jesus' many miracles. John used the word *sign*, *sēmeíon*—a sign (typically miraculous) given especially to confirm, corroborate, or authenticate.[2] John recorded these signs because they were meant to authenticate Jesus as the Son of God; that's right, the *Son of God*! Signs are so incredible and stunning that they can only be attributed to the Messiah.

We must understand the magnitude of Jesus' miracles to have perspective on our lives and the miracles He wants to perform in our relationships. We need a reimagined imagination to grasp the miracles of Jesus. Many people today have had their imaginations suffocated or withered by misuse or lack of use. Through the enemy's influence (Satan), our culture's enticement (the world), and the lust of our flesh, we succumb to the use of our imagination on perversions and distractions. Sin renders us incapable of imagining the beauty and supremacy of God. Our inability to be still, in silence and peace, robs us of the time required to observe God's majestic creation and its inexhaustible possibilities.

As I listen to others, it is evident that many people simply can't imagine what it would be like to have peace in their lives. They see a mountain of broken relationships as overwhelming, unscalable, and impossible to deal with—particularly those with family members. They simply throw up their hands because they can't envision the miraculous hand of God intervening in their brokenness. Many of you are saying to yourself right now, "It would take a miracle from God to be reunited with some of my past friends or relatives."

God wants to reimage your imagination so that you can see into the unseen and picture what life would be like with peace and restoration in your relationships. If you can see this possibility, it will create an insatiable longing in you.

Consider this contrast, seeing life in:

- Black and white, or
- VFX (Filmmakers see use visual effects to create imagery that does not exist in the real physical world and add in 3D, perceiving sound from every direction, including above and below you.)

Think about this new way of seeing; it will prime your imagination as we contemplate miraculous things that few people have ever seen. And what is even more breathtaking is that it takes you into the realm that does exist, the realm of the Holy Spirit—where all things are possible, where forgiveness and reconciliation flourish.

Imagine yourself in the following dreams and visions: observing, feeling, and smelling these encounters. Feel the pulsing of your heartbeat as the sounds of these visions and dreams encircle you.

In chapter 1 of Ezekiel, the prophet is allowed to see the throne of God, but it is not what we would expect it to be. He sees a fireball, a whirlwind with a raging fire, and living beings that have human forms but four faces and four wings. The beings run to and fro like lightning bolts while they carry wheels. Then Ezekiel sees it—the appearance of the likeness of the glory of God. Are you ready to scream, "Get me out of here!" I would be.

In Isaiah chapter 6, Isaiah encounters God in His holy temple. He sees the Lord God of heaven sitting on the throne and converses with Him. But before the conversation took place, something had to happen to Isaiah: His unclean lips had to be made clean and his sins forgiven. Hold on to your seat with both hands. The next scene is one of Scripture's most staggering and frightening encounters. He sees seraphim (beings mentioned only once in Scripture, here). Remember that new imagination? You will need all of it right now. Picture six-winged beings flying around with four wings covering their faces and crying out, "Holy, Holy, Holy, is the Lord of armies. The whole earth is full of His glory" (Isa. 6:3, NASB). As the seraphim fly and shout, the temple's foundation shakes and smoke fills the air. Then it happens—one of the most spectacular exchanges in the Bible. A seraph grabs a burning coal from the altar, places it on Isaiah's lips, and declares that his iniquity is taken away and his sins are forgiven. Now, that will stretch your imagination.

I could go on with dreams and visions from the Scriptures. Read Revelation 1:12-18 on your own. But let me share a vision I had.

I woke in the night weeping with tears running down my cheeks. I thought I was awake and then realized I was asleep and having a vision in my dreams. Standing in the front row of our church, I saw an angel; I knew it was Gabriel, and he had his eyes directly on me. He was speaking to me but not in words. He told me the Holy Spirit was sending a refreshing—a new anointing—on my life to be an ambassador for Christ. I was weeping as he spoke, and I fell to the ground. It was then I understood his face and eyes showed on every side of his body, and I realized that the angel wasn't just speaking to me but everyone in the congregation.

The Greater Miracle

You have just read accounts of miracles, visions, and dreams. But let's consider an even greater miracle, that greatest of miracles.

Is there any more remarkable miracle in our physical world than the birth of a baby? The human conception, development, and birth process is as enigmatic as it is unexplainable. Thousands of sperm swim through obstacles to reach an egg that only one will enter, and when it does, the egg stealthily seals out all the others. The embryo, its development and birth, breathing and language formation, are all so, so...words do fail! Nothing in the physical realm gives us a more precise snapshot of the miraculous working of the God of the universe than the birth and maturation of a baby. And conversely, nothing reveals to us more distinctly the ugly, demonic forces of Satan on earth than abortion.

I've heard doctors talk about this unrecognizable blob of fetal tissue that begins in the womb and becomes a separate, unique human being. How does that happen? The truth is many doctors are fascinated and have no explanation. Except for this one conclusion: *it is all accidental, a freak of evolution*. Can you swallow that?

Nova is the most-watched science television series in the world. Seen in over one hundred countries, it is also the most-watched documentary series on PBS. And Nova's most-watched documentary ever is *The Miracle of Life* (1982)."[3] Why? The miracle of creation through birth is simply mesmerizing.

And Now the New Birth

Jesus comes along and says, "You must be born again." Born again? A second miraculous birth would be the miracle of all miracles.

Jesus answered him, "Truly, truly I say to you, unless a man is born again, he cannot see the kingdom of God." Nicodemus said to Him, "How can a man be born when he is old? Can he enter a second time into his mother's womb and be born?" Jesus answered, "Truly, truly I say to you, unless a man is born of water and the Spirit, he cannot enter the kingdom of God. That which is born of the flesh is flesh, and that which is born of the Spirit is spirit. Do not marvel that I said to you, 'You must be born again.' The wind blows where it wishes, and you hear its sound, but you do not know where it comes from or where it goes. So it is with everyone who is born of the Spirit." Nicodemus said to Him, "How can this be?"

—John 3:3-9

Unless a man is born again he cannot see the kingdom of God (John 3:3). What could Jesus have meant with these words for Nicodemus—the learned scholar, teacher of the law, and ruler of the Jews? Nicodemus, in a typical pharisaical response, proceeded to press Jesus with a rebuttal: "Can he enter a second time into his mother's womb and be born?" (John 3:4) When Jesus answers Nicodemus' question and says a man must be born of water and the Spirit to enter the kingdom of God, He loses Nicodemus completely. Nicodemus responds, "How can these things be" (John 3:9b, NASB)?

Because Jesus was full of the Holy Spirit and thoroughly united with the Father, He lived, spoke, and walked daily in the realm of the kingdom, the realm of the Spirit. Jesus said things that were perfectly foreign to the natural mind. He proposed things, as in this instance with Nicodemus, that were as confusing as they were out of the question. Nicodemus, like all Pharisees, was stuck in the transitory human understanding.

He Is Speaking; Are You Listening?

Jesus is speaking to you and me today as pointedly as to Nicodemus in this passage so many centuries ago. Jesus describes the miracle of all miracles, an event more extraordinary than any vision we could have or any miracle He performed in the Gospels. Jesus describes the new birth, a heart being made new, and the spirit of man being made alive to God. It is the most incredible transformation and only accomplished through the power of the Holy Spirit. It cannot be wrought by the wisdom or power that man has. "I will give you a new heart and put a new spirit in you; I will remove from you your heart of stone and give you a heart of flesh" (Ezek. 36:26, NIV).

Here's the deal. Jesus performed so many miracles. They had a purpose—to convince others that He was the Messiah. Jesus continually emphasizes the healing of the spirit of man, the healing of bitterness and hostility and lust and anger and worry and anxiety and a critical spirit. He is after this: deliverance from these ugly and evil things. Christ wants us free to experience fellowship with one another, and these vile things stand in the way.

But let's make this very personal, where it intersects your life.

Is God big enough to perform the great miracle of changing your heart and healing your broken relationships? Do you have a supernatural imagination sufficient to see this in the unseen?

Our heart is the issue, these hearts from which come evil thoughts, murder, adultery, all sexual immorality, theft, lying, slander, and gossip (Matt. 15:19). Just the sound of that last word, *gossip*, has such a malignant aura.

When it comes to the broken relationships in our families, the separation from Christian friends, and the explosion of division in Christ's church, I believe we are striving to find answers without recognizing the one obvious, overlooked solution. The answer is the miraculous power of God to change our hearts.

The transformation of our hearts begins with repentance. Repentance takes me out of my small self and brings me to the foot of the cross, where I find forgiveness. Repentance speaks to my conscious life—where unforgiveness lives, disunity breeds, and irreconcilable differences germinate and fester.

Without true repentance, there can never be peace among men or women; there will always be strife. However, if we are born of the Spirit, the very nature of Christ begins to work in us. The wall between us and others can be obliterated with Christ. What is that wall? Our egos and pride. We can come to others through Jesus because He is the Prince of Peace. "For He is our peace, who has made both groups one and has broken down the barrier of the dividing wall" (Eph. 2:14).

The One Gate

The Christian way has only one entrance gate; once there, there is only one roadway. The small gate of entry is repentance. And much to our chagrin and disbelief, the roadway is narrow. It gets more alarming. Few enter the gate and find the way that leads to life (Matt. 7:13-14). The way is reserved for those who become increasingly like little children—obeying the Father out of adoration, love, and fear. Yes, fear. I will elaborate much more on this later.

Repentance is the gateway; no other portal exists to the kingdom of heaven.

The message of repentance is as elementary as the gospel gets. In the Gospel of Mark, Mark skips all the stories about Jesus' birth and ancestry and immediately dives into the heart of the gospel. The messenger has come to prepare the way for the Messiah, delivering one word: repent and be baptized.

The beginning of the gospel of Jesus Christ, the Son of God. As it is written in the Prophets: "Look, I am sending My messenger before Your face, who will prepare Your way before You. The voice of one crying in the wilderness: 'Prepare the way of the Lord, make His paths straight.' John came baptizing in the wilderness and preaching a baptism of repentance for the remission of sins."

—Mark 1:1-4

And very quickly, Mark affirms that the message of repentance is the message of Jesus, the Messiah. The first thing that Jesus commands sinners to do is repent.

After John was put in prison, Jesus came to Galilee preaching the gospel of the kingdom of God, saying, "The time is fulfilled, and the kingdom of God is at hand. Repent and believe the gospel."

—Mark 1:14

Through this joyous deforming and reforming repentance, our hard hearts are made alive to God, and we come to our spiritual senses. We grieve and cry over that one thing worth suffering over: sin. Oh, what our sin costs others—the pain, tears, and wreckage.

I had an uncle who went from a star college golfer and baseball player to a police captain and highly successful CPA to being in federal prison. His marriage failed. He spent most of his adult life in maximum-security prisons for fencing high-end diamonds. He was separated and divided from family and friends.

When Jim finally exited prison late in his sixties, he repented and eventually married a wonderful, godly woman. He was full of joy and delight. He had been imprisoned in darkness for decades and was now saved by the grace of Christ Jesus. He lived the last years of his life in peace, reconnecting with family and friends. Jim's heart was alive to God. Forgiveness flowed to and from Jim.

In repentance, we are one of the many prisoners enslaved to sin who are now set free by the greatness of God's compassion and Christ's sacrifice. Nothing can surpass the joy of having our wrongdoings wiped out by the cleansing blood of Christ. It is not hard for me to imagine the utter joy and freedom my Uncle Jim basked in during his later years; there are few places darker than prison. I also have been freed from the prison of sinful strongholds. In our utter hopelessness, addictions, and sentence of death, Jesus comes and sets us free.

But let me be clear. This joyful, reforming salvation doesn't transform us into sainthood. Salvation does not cure our sinful propensities once and for all. We don't blithely forgive everyone who has ever wronged or offended us. And we don't wake up one morning immune to the offenses of life. No! All of us are called to enter into the most perfect worship we can offer to our Savior, offering our bodies as a living sacrifice (Rom. 12:1-2). With salvation intact, we come face to face every day with the choices that will take us down the road of discipleship and sanctification—the road of transformation. Thank God we have the Holy Spirit to guide, empower, correct, and keep us on course.

And while I'm at it, let me emphatically confront the notion that we behave our way into the kingdom of heaven. Salvation is a miracle of grace, and righteousness is a gift from God received by faith. God isn't waiting until we get our act together so He can bestow on us His righteousness. As we receive His righteousness, we are freed from our brokenness. All this freedom comes to us through the power of God's Holy Spirit.

I will instruct you and teach you in the way you should go; I will advise you with My eye upon you.

—Psalm 32:8, NASB

Whether St. Augustine, Paul, you, or me, we all live in the same state: the need for daily repentance. St. Augustine of Hippo was a theologian, philosopher, and the Bishop of Hippo Regius in North Africa. His life and writings had a momentous influence on Western Christianity. He was the dominant personality and thinker of Christian antiquity. Yet this church giant penned this simple prayer of his need for repentance and forgiveness in his book *Confessions.*

> O Lord, the house of my soul is narrow; enlarge it that thou mayest enter in. It is ruinous, O repair it! It displeases thy sight; I confess it, I know. But who shall cleanse it, or to whom shall I cry but thee? Cleanse me from my secret faults, O Lord, and spare thy servant from strange sins.

—ST. AUGUSTINE, *Confessions*[4]

This is the cleansing we must have—this cleaning from criticism and judgments, those and other strange, often hidden sins that separate us from others. Every day we are tempted to think ill of others and criticize people because they do not walk through life perfectly or meet our expectations. And those ugly criticisms are just as powerful to injure when unspoken, breaking us apart from others.

Nothing will strangle our spiritual life more thoroughly and leave us as susceptible to a divisive spirit as a lack of daily repentance. Without the lifestyle of repentance, we become complacent and unaware of our attitudes of superiority and indifference to the body of Christ, and worst of all, our hearts become hardened. Without daily repentance and obedience, we can become easily deceived into thinking we have arrived at some place of spirituality. In reality, we may be in the "kingdom of gray," and the white and black of sin becomes indiscernible. Our capacity for self-deception is shocking. I challenge you with this dire warning: If you do not live daily in repentance, you are vulnerable to the enemy's subtle schemes. Every day without repentance is a day for pride to fester and grow like a grossly infected boil.

Eugene Peterson put it aptly in light of our instant society fixated on quick fixes with the title of his book *A Long Obedience in the Same Direction: Discipleship in an Instant Society.* I often hear this title quoted from people who understand the importance of following Jesus daily.

So this is what we do: We repeatedly return to the cross. We kneel, and Jesus forgives us and keeps us clean. At the end of the day, we examine ourselves and ask the Holy Spirit where we won and where we lost. God's Holy Spirit is our spiritual cleansing agent.

Walking in repentance and forgiveness is not an easy thing. If it was, there would be much more harmony in the body of Christ. No! Authentic, godly repentance is a demanding thing. It can never be flippant or easily achieved. It cannot be glazed over with sugar-coated words as we quickly move on to the next task. True repentance is a rare thing. There are concrete signs of godly repentance, not the least of which are assuming responsibility for our actions, forgiving others, and activating restitution when needed.

The kingdom of heaven and this great miracle of a new heart are built on the foundation of repentance. True repentance will always produce the fruit of humility. Humility is the ointment that can heal broken relationships and birth reconciliation.

Take a quiet moment here and reflect on the greatness of God and His miraculous work in your heart.

CHAPTER 3

FORGIVENESS: THE OIL OF THE SPIRIT

The deepest things are often comprehended by the simple
mind, and the profound can be apprehended by the child.[1]

—ANNIE JOHNSON FLINT

Before diving into forgiveness, I have a story about someone who died recently. Very few people know him outside of family members. He will never be canonized for sainthood, although his life and actions may validate him to have been recognized as one. He attended a Christian secondary school and graduated from a Bible college. He wrote many books, none of which have been or will ever be published. He was a man of the Word and led many to Christ as a bold witness. He prayed for everyone he encountered (this is not an exaggeration.) He was afflicted and persecuted because of the Word but did not fall away (he was the good soil of Matthew 13:19-23). I weep as I write, as did everyone at his funeral, but not tears of sadness; instead, tears for the fondness with which everyone remembers a true warrior for Jesus—one who lived out the prayer of Saint Ignatius of Loyola.

Dear Lord teach me to be generous; teach me to serve you as you deserve, to give and not to count the cost, to fight and not to heed the wounds, to toil and not to seek for rest, to labor and not to ask for reward, save that of knowing that I do your will. Amen.[2]

Loren suffered from learning disabilities and other challenges early in life. In his late teen years, he was diagnosed with a major mental illness (schizophrenia), which he would struggle with for the remainder of his life, dying at age fifty-two.

Loren lived on his own but briefly, and for the last ten years he was in a group home. Having endured many, many shock treatments during in-patient care, abused, and marginalized, Loren suffered as few have. I could wax on about his spirituality, dedication, and zeal for Jesus; it never waned through any trials.

I possess one of Loren's books, titled *How to Be Set Free in Him*. I hope you enjoy these first two pages of chapter 1, "How to Get Joy in Your Life." And I pray these simple pages prick your heart over what Loren writes: "We cannot have his Joy in our lives unless we love ourselves like are neighbor."

Chapter one - How to get joy in your life.

We are to enjoy the people in one live and have a life of joy in one life. Do not allow one problems to get us down.

Proverbs 14:30 - a sound or right heart comes to get one body down But envy or jealous is as rotteness to one bones. If we dont have a pure heart before him then we cannot have joy in one life Dont allow the enemy to keep you to a wrong heart that has sin in your life so you will not be set free in him. If we dont keep one life by reading his word and praying daily then we cannot be set free in him. Dont allow the enemy keep you in

we cannot have his joy in our lives unless we stay right with him. we cannot have his joy in our lives unless we love ourselves like are neighbor.

Romans 12:18 - But we need to live peaceabely with all men if we do not allow his word to change our lives and allow him to take us to be more like him

Hebrews 12:14 - we are to pursue or go after it him and our peace with all people and his holiness without no one will see the Lord. we cannot walk in peace unless we seek him and dwell in him.

Romans 12:21 - we are to overcome or have victory in him But we are to overcome evil with good. If someone wrongs us then we need to stay with him to follow at peace and learn him in all are ways.

DISCLAIMER   DISCLAIMER   DISCLAIMER

No magic pill, formula, prayer, study course, book, or other means can guarantee forgiveness and its benefits. Forgiveness is often a personal experience and must fit the very shape of your soul—a shape like no one else.

Forgiveness is not linear, not at a specific point in time. It must be revisited relentlessly and on many occasions. Our emotions are crucial in forgiveness and are not turned on and off like a water spigot.

C. S. Lewis wrote, "I note with great displeasure that your patient has become a Christian. There is no need to despair; hundreds of these adult converts have been reclaimed after a brief sojourn in the Enemy's camp and are now with us. All the habits of the patient, both mental and bodily, are still in our favor."[3] All the habits. It sounds like an obituary—that is what the enemy of your soul desires to achieve. The devil hopes that we, like dogs, return to the vomit of sin and our habits and that one most destructive practice: living with unforgiveness.

Unforgiveness is that nasty state of being in which resentment, offense, and bitterness fester in our souls. Unforgiveness is often driven by vengeance (I'll cover this more in chapter 9). Unforgiveness unchecked defiles every sinew of our being; we deceive ourselves into thinking we can live the everyday Christian life with it. However, unforgiveness renders us powerless—like so many others, imprisoned—though we may not recognize it, and foulest of all, we end up religious. We smile as if everything is good; we think it is. It isn't!

The sojourn of following Jesus begins with receiving His forgiveness for our sins (1 John 1:9). For most of us, this encounter produces joy like no joy we have known before. It exceeds the glorious sunrise in sixty-eight-degree weather on the most magnificent beach on the planet—on steroids. Christ cleanses us from our wrongdoings and evil deeds; we have a new heart and spirit. We experience that miracle of miracles, a second birth.

But the most startling property of this new life is that it sought us out. It found us. He chose us. Christ doesn't choose us based on our potential, beauty, education, social standing, or physical prowess. We are chosen because God loved us first. When I look at the beautiful sky—the mystical stars, the eternal, unending universe, and the realization that the Creator of all this loves and chose me—it is beyond my senses and understanding.

But being chosen by God (John 15:16) is far from the end of the story. Instead, it's the beginning. Christ Jesus calls us to be disciples and work out our salvation. Reconciled to God, we have become His conduit on earth—His eyes, feet, and hands. Through us, He makes this glorious salvation known to sinners. "We are therefore Christ's ambassadors, as though God were making his appeal through us. We implore you on Christ's behalf: Be reconciled to God" (2 Cor. 5:20, NIV).

Gerald Hopkins, the English poet and Jesuit priest, masterfully and vividly expressed this thought: We are Christ's ambassadors. He lives through us in the world. Hopkins writes of this in the latter part of his poem, *As Kingfishers Catch Fire.*

> *I say móre: the just man justices;*
> *Keeps grace: thát keeps all his goings graces;*
> *Acts in God's eye what in God's eye he is—*
> *Christ—for Christ plays in ten thousand places,*
> *Lovely in limbs, and lovely in eyes not his*
> *To the Father through the features of men's faces.*[4]

The key, which is our repentance and God's forgiveness, has opened the small gate for us (Matt. 7:13-14). We have embarked on the narrow path, the path avoided by the crowd. The narrow way is not an easy road. If anyone tells you that following Jesus is trouble-free and effortless, they are either not following Jesus, are lying to you, or live in deception. Following Jesus is entering the war, spiritual warfare. We draw the sword of the Word to rebuff the world, bring bloody death to our flesh (self and pride), and slay the enemy—Satan and his demons. N. T. Wright, theologian, author of more than seventy books, and Bishop of Durham, puts it this way, "Never let it be said that the Christian faith is an airy-fairy thing."[5]

Forgiveness is a complex affair. Where do I begin? So many significant engagements must be fought in this battle to live in forgiveness. However, the enemy draws us away from crucial battles with cunning devices. He hoodwinks us into minor skirmish after skirmish that has little to do with the fight to become mature followers of Jesus. We battle the spiritual and emotional clashes that have negligible impacts on us taking our rightful place as His ambassadors in the land. We major in outward habits. Do you drink? Is your hair too long? Her pants are too tight! We scrutinize the minor. Were you at church last week? I think she has a tattoo. Did they go to *that* movie? In his prayer, David recognizes the devil's wiles: "Protect me from their evil scheming, from all their demonic subterfuge" (Ps. 141:9, MSG).

In his cloak-and-dagger attacks, the enemy diverts our attention from the critical encounters, the difference makers; there is none so crucial and daunting as forgiveness—forgiving others and seeking forgiveness when we err or offend. Forgiveness is simply tough stuff; it explains why there are so many attritions from the narrow road. There are few things the church so grossly underestimates as the significance of forgiveness. The enemy has released spiritual nerve gas and blinded us to the truth: We must live in forgiveness toward all people. It is not optional—right-sizing the implications of this principal battleground forgiveness. It becomes one of the most vicious fights we will encounter in our quest to follow Jesus. God's essential purpose of seeing unity in His body is the reward for this victory.

How significant is this battle to live in forgiveness toward others? Your soul's eternal resting place is the outcome of this engagement. Does that help you comprehend the importance of living in forgiveness? Be ye reconciled. It is Jesus' heart cry and what He desires for all His children.

How can one aspect of the Christian life be so crucial? How can success be so intense and the battle rage so fierce?

The answer is simple. Forgiveness is the oil of the Spirit. Let me explain.

The Oil

When teaching our children to drive, most of us stress the importance of *not* running out of gas. There are few more annoying and unnecessary disturbances than that late-night call from a child, "I'm out of gas." Of course, I am sure God must be somewhere in this conversation. Perhaps you had been praying for patience. Facetiousness aside, the car is a marvelous example of the essential lesson in following Jesus—right-sizing the necessity of forgiveness.

One essential lesson stopped the show when I instructed my children, goddaughters, and grandchildren on driving. You must never continue to run the car when the oil light comes on. There are very few lessons that happen to you one time and you learn the moral of the story for the rest of your life. Running out of oil in a car and continuing to drive will lead to that lifetime learning experience. I learned from my lesson with a little Volkswagen at age nineteen; the oil light came on, and I didn't stop. Oh, I came to a stop! Ten miles farther down the road, my motor was smoking, blown, and unrepairable, as the mechanic informed me later.

Forgiveness is the oil that lubricates the journey with Christ and keeps it operating smoothly. It allows us to move forward, not be static or frozen in time. Without forgiveness, our walk with Jesus is turbulent, sorrowful, and full of conflict. The Christian life quickly becomes powerless and nonthreatening to the enemy when we live with unforgiveness. Our walk with Jesus eventually blows up like that VW engine. In contrast, the more God's incredible forgiveness engulfs us, the thinner the space between heaven and earth. The joy of the Lord becomes our strength; we encounter the peace of God in our relationships, and the power of the Holy Spirit is alive in us.

But we have a troubling problem assimilating forgiveness because we have not followed God's instructions or standards. We have followed the world's lead. Most Christians are perfectly comfortable with having a trail of broken relationships behind them. Just go ahead and admit it; this toleration of division is not what the Bible teaches.

We are to forgive others as we have been forgiven.

Think with me about someone who has deeply hurt you to the very core of your heart. These are all representations of stories I am aware of:

- That confidence you shared with your closest friend; she repeats your secret sins to others.

- A colleague gains your confidence over months and becomes a good friend (you think). But you discover they were secretly gaining information against you to use when they petitioned management for promotion above you.

- After years of faithful service in youth ministry, you ask for a chance to participate on the worship team (you have musical experience and gifts). The worship director flippantly dismisses you and tells you to try another church if you want to sing so badly. Oh, and this is the church your whole family attends.

- One of your siblings has taken advantage of your elderly parents and pilfered over half of what would have been your inheritance.

- You discover your strict and puritanical mother has had a secret lover for years while married to your kind and loving father. Oh, and you find out you have a half-sister you never knew about.

Of course, these examples could go on and on, *ad nauseum*. And I am sure, dear reader, that you can add examples that carry more profound and even more devastating hurts with disgusting outcomes. Yet we are still left with this standard that Jesus set for forgiveness: It knows no boundaries. "And when you stand praying, forgive if you have anything against anyone, so that your Father who is in heaven may also forgive you your sins" (Mark 11:25).

What do we do with "other-worldly" forgiveness from God? Let's contrast what we too often do with what God says.

- "And I will forgive their wickedness, and I will never again remember their sins" (Heb. 8:12, NLT).

  > We may eventually forgive someone, but we swear we will never forget what they did to us.

- "Dear friends, never take revenge. Leave that to the righteous anger of God. For the Scriptures say, 'I will take revenge; I will pay them back,' says the LORD" (Rom. 12:19, NLT).

  > We call down the wrath of God on someone who has sinned against our family or us.

- "Then Peter came to Him and said, 'Lord, how often shall I forgive my brother who sins against me? Up to seven times?' Jesus said to him, 'I do not say to you up to seven times, but up to seventy times seven'" (Matt. 18:21-22).

  > Forgive? Sure, I'll forgive them once or twice, but after that I've learned my lesson about that person.

- "Do good to those who hate you. Bless those who curse you. Pray for those who hurt you" (Luke 6:27b, 28, NLT).

  > Instead of responding with kindness when another person hurts us, we withdraw from them. We warn anyone who will listen to be wary of them.

Forgiveness Is the Tipping Point

There are only a few things you must get right in the Christian faith. Forgiveness is premier in that small cluster of items we must enthusiastically embrace. Read the following paragraphs closely and slowly.

I believe forgiveness is less complicated than what many theologians and ministers of the gospel present. The gospel's simplicity is outrageous. It scandalizes our minds. Joyce Meyers said it best: "Forgiveness is not a feeling—it's a decision we make because we want to do what's right before God. It's a quality decision that won't be easy and may take time to get through the process, depending on the severity of the offense."[6] That's it.

Jesus has made forgiveness the simple and dramatic tipping point in the Christian life. Everything can and does hinge on this one issue: how we forgive others. And Jesus didn't just drop this bomb on His disciples and move on to the next teaching or revelation. He reinforced this concept of forgiveness with the disciples time and again. He presents it in such straightforward language that it is indefensible and timeless.

We think, wait a minute; this is outlandish. Could Jesus have meant what He said?

But it is time for a crucial gut check—Jesus means what He says in the Word. He doesn't say things haphazardly. He is *the* Man of truth. There can be no doubt Jesus is delivering one of the gospel's fundamental, pivotal messages: If you don't forgive, you won't be forgiven. How fundamental is this in Jesus' thinking? Consider this.

The Disciple's Prayer

Throughout history, there have been majestic prayers that are recognized worldwide: The Instrument of Your Peace—St. Francis of Assisi; the Serenity Prayer—Reinhold Niebuhr; Christ Be with Me—St. Patrick; and John Wesley's Covenant and Baptismal Covenant. There are more, but none rivals the instant identification, popularity, and daily recitation of the Lord's Prayer.

Jesus' disciples came to Him after realizing the significance of prayer in His life. They saw Him begin and end His day in prayer. He prayed about everything. They wanted what He had. John the Baptist had taught some of his disciples to pray, so Jesus' disciples asked Him to teach them to pray. The Lord's Prayer, which Jesus taught the disciples to pray, has had volumes of books written about it throughout history. The prayer is used by almost all Christian churches with few exceptions. It is the prayer of all prayers.

The disciple's prayer has four central points: We pray for God's purposes, for provision, for pardon, and for protection. Only one of these themes has a condition attached to it.

Jesus tells the disciples to pray this way, "And forgive us our debts, as we forgive our debtors" (Matt. 6:12, KJV). That little word, *as*, bears more discussion and confirms what is a life-altering revelation to us about forgiveness. *As* (*hōs*) is an adverb of comparative, which how, i.e., In the manner of.[7] What Jesus is saying in the most instructive, far-reaching, and noteworthy prayer in the history of humans is: You will receive forgiveness in the same manner you forgive others.

This understanding that forgiveness must be given to others if we want forgiveness is the centerpiece and the only course for healing broken relationships. Judgment always begins with the household of God, and we are responsible before God to walk in forgiveness toward others. It is God's divine purpose.

Unforgiveness Is a Sin

Unforgiveness is a sin that opens the door to the enemy's work in our lives, leading to the inevitable fruit of bitterness. The Bible has plenty to say about bitterness and gives pointed warnings. "Pursue peace with all men, and the holiness without which no one will see the Lord, watching diligently so that no one falls short of the grace of God, lest any root of bitterness spring up to cause trouble, and many become defiled by it" (Heb. 12:14-15).

Picture in your mind's eye someone taking a big drink of poison, thinking it will relieve the offense or pain another person caused them. This is what bitterness looks like. Marianne Williamson is famously quoted as saying, "Unforgiveness is like drinking poison yourself and waiting for the other person to die."[8] In Deuteronomy 32, God judges Israel for abandoning His covenant with them rather than seeking forgiveness. Moses likens the wine they have chosen to drink to grapes of poison, bitter clusters from the venom of serpents and cobras. "Their vine comes from the vine of Sodom and from the fields of Gomorrah. Their grapes are filled with poison, and their clusters with bitterness. Their wine is the venom of serpents, the deadly poison of cobras" (Deut. 32:32-33).

When Peter rebuked Simon the magician for thinking he could buy the anointing of the Holy Spirit, Peter recognized Simon had become bitter and full of sin. "For I see that you are full of bitterness and captive to sin" (Acts 8:23, NIV). Bitter is the Greek word *pikra*; it means the gall of bitterness and extreme wickedness.[9] It's the same word Paul uses in Romans 3:14, "Their mouths are full of cursing and bitterness" (NIV).

Peace with others is the goal. Unforgiveness is the mountain in the road, creating an impasse to right relationships. It comes down to this: The unforgiving person has set themselves up as God. Unknowingly, they have taken inside their heart a poison pill that will defile and eventually destroy them.

Good Ending

Everyone likes a good story; few Bible stories are more well-known than the unforgiving enslaved person in Matthew 18:23-35. At first blush, it is a compelling story about forgiving others: an enslaved person who owes so much money to the king and can't repay it, and the king eventually forgives his debt. How positive and marvelous. That enslaved person turns right around and calls in debt owed to him by another enslaved person. A debt minuscule in comparison to his debt—bad slave. The king discovers what the servant has done and rescinds his debt cancellation—a seemingly good story.

But the conclusion of the story bears no resemblance to a nice, docile story about the importance of forgiveness. The ending of this tale is spine-chilling, breathtaking, and bloodcurdling.

Bad Ending

Therefore, the kingdom of heaven is like a king who wanted to settle accounts with his servants. As he began the settlement, a man who owed him ten thousand bags of gold was brought to him. Since he was not able to pay, the master ordered that he and his wife and his children and all that he had to be sold to repay the debt. At this, the servant fell on his knees before him. "Be patient with me," he begged, "and I will pay back everything." The servant's master took pity on him, canceled the debt and let him go.

But when that servant went out, he found one of his fellow servants who owed him a hundred silver coins. He grabbed him and began to choke him. "Pay back what you owe me!" he demanded. His fellow servant fell to his knees and begged him, "Be patient with me, and I will pay it back." But he refused. Instead, he went off and had the man thrown into prison until he could pay the debt. When the other servants saw what had happened, they were outraged and went and told their master everything that had happened. Then, the master called the servant in. "You wicked servant," he said, "I canceled all that debt of yours because you begged me to. Shouldn't you have had mercy on your fellow servant just as I had on you?" In anger his master handed him over to the jailers to be tortured, until he should pay back all he owed. "This is how my heavenly Father will treat each of you unless you forgive your brother or sister from your heart."

—Matthew 18:23-35, NIV

To get a handle on the enormity of the king's forgiveness of the first enslaved person, we need to understand the size of the debt. And we must compare what the second enslaved person owed the first. "The debt, 10,000 talents, is 200,000 years of labor! It is 60,000,000 working days. The second servant owed 100 denarii to the first servant, which is a significant sum. It's four months wages."[10] Two hundred thousand years of labor compared to four months. You can do the math; the difference is astronomical.

But here is where the story takes a twist that should give us great pause and solemnity. When the king discovers the first servant had thrown the second servant in prison over his comparably infinitesimal debt, the king declares him wicked and turns him over to the torturers. That's right, torturers!

In many of the stories (parables) Jesus tells, He does not give the interpretation. Yet in this parable He leaves nothing to be misconstrued. "This is how my heavenly Father will treat each of you unless you forgive your brother or sister from your heart" (Matt. 18:35, NIV).

All the excuses in the world count as nothing in the eyes of God when it comes to forgiveness: betrayals, gossip, theft, assaults—the list is as endless as man's debauchery. In all of this, God has grace. "And God is able to bless you abundantly, so that in all things at all times, having all that you need, you will abound in every good work" (2 Cor. 9:8, NIV).

There is little in life more challenging than to issue forgiveness to someone who has purposely tried to destroy you. But you must act now to forgive; eternity hangs in the balance.

Eternity: "endless life after death."[11]

Forgiveness and restoration are God's essence. They are His constant state. Forgiveness is the oil of the Spirit that smooths the way for unity. Perfect unity is paramount to God.

"I have given them the glory which You gave Me, that they may be one even as We are one: I in them and You in Me, that they may be perfect in unity, and that the world may know that You have sent Me, and have loved them as You have loved Me" (John 17:22-23).

Where do you stand on this forgiveness continuum?

- You are forgiving all who have harmed you and seeking to mend broken relationships. And as far as it depends on you, you have done everything possible to live in peace with everyone, and I mean everyone the Holy Spirit has brought to your remembrance.

Or:

- You have refused to forgive. You are unbending, insisting on your way. The other person is wrong, and they need to pay for it (vindication). There are people you refuse to forgive. You know little of the cross of Christ if this is the case. There are corridors of your heart that you have never allowed the Holy Spirit to enter.

"Forgiveness," says Bible teacher Warren Wiersbe, "is the greatest miracle Jesus ever performs. It meets the greatest need. It costs the greatest price. And it brings the greatest blessing and the most lasting results."[12]

CHAPTER 4

BAD THEOLOGY

Imagine yourself as a living house. God comes in to rebuild that house. At first, perhaps, you can understand what He is doing. You thought you were going to be made into a decent little cottage: but He is building a palace. He intends to come and live in it Himself.[1]

—C. S. LEWIS

One of my first mentors, Dr. Charles Farah, often said, "Bad theology is a cruel taskmaster." Theology, simply put, is what you believe about God from your study of Him.[2] And the truth is that if you don't get your theology right when the storms of life come—and they come to all of us—you will succumb. You will not be able to withstand the violent attacks of the enemy and the traumas of living in this fallen world.

When building a house, there is nothing more frustrating or disappointing (or as staggeringly expensive) as having to fix foundation problems. Those problems will affect everything inside and outside the house and everyone living there. That is the way with bad theology. If you view your life like a spiritual house, the foundation of that house is your belief system and theology.

I wanted to impress my oldest grandson with the importance of building your spiritual life on the proper foundation. It just so happened that Isaac's other grandfather, Dr. Lloyd, was getting ready to break ground on constructing a medical clinic with his doctor son, my son-in-law. It is from the riches of God's grace that Lloyd and I are squarely on the same page spiritually about our grandchildren.

Lloyd and I concocted a plan to drive this spiritual lesson deep into Isaac's ten-year-old brain. From the backhoe digging the first trench and putting his hands in the dirt, to seeing the setting of the rebar (the steel bars embedded in poured concrete footings to make them stronger), to the actual pouring of the concrete, Isaac would get to see firsthand every step involved in the making of a strong foundation. Isaac would watch the walls go up on that foundation, the roof constructed, the flooring laid, and all the finishers do their jobs. I wanted Isaac to see that everything depends on the strength of a rightly built foundation. What a lesson! Dr. Lloyd has pictures to remind Isaac of this.

Jesus also taught about foundations. He concluded the most crucial teaching of His time on earth, the Sermon on the Mount, with a majestic parable. In this parable, Jesus instructs His followers about the importance of a proper foundation.

Whoever hears these sayings of Mine and does them, I will liken him to a wise man who built his house on a rock. And the rain descended, the floods came, and the winds blew and beat on that house. And it did not fall, for it was founded on a rock. And everyone who hears these sayings of Mine and does not do them will be likened to a foolish man who built his house on the sand. And the rain descended, the floods came, and the winds blew and beat on that house. And it fell. And its fall was great.

—Matthew 7:24-27

This story about the wise man and the foolish man offers two starkly contrasting examples of what happens when construction goes awry with the foundation. Both houses may have looked pristine from the outside, had the most expensive finishing materials of the day in and out, the finest amenities for comfort, and state-of-the-art waterproofing to withstand storms. The two men built similar houses with only one distinguishing difference: the foundation.

Almost everyone I ask about this parable and what the foundation represents gives me a similar response: We are to build our house on Jesus, the rock. Their answer is precisely what I learned years ago in my little country Baptist Sunday school class: that song, "The wise man built his house upon the rock."

So build your life on the Lord Jesus Christ
So build your life on the Lord Jesus Christ.
So build your life on the Lord Jesus Christ
And the blessings come tumbling down.[3]

However, the conclusions I have heard from others about this parable are different from what I believe Jesus is teaching. Jesus is teaching one simple, paramount idea. He addresses two very similar men who hear His words; the only difference is that one obeys, the other does not. Jesus makes it emphatically clear: "Whoever hears these sayings of Mine and does them is wise" (Matt. 7:24). "And everyone who hears these sayings of Mine and does not do them is foolish" (Matt. 7:26).

Jesus' parable demonstrates the outcome of not obeying His teachings. The storms of life will expose you to destruction, and if you have a family, they will be swept away too. Jesus could not be more direct and unmistakable.

The parable of the two men who built houses that looked the same on the outside is sobering and should give us pause. We must get our theology right about forgiveness and obey God's commands. Forgiveness toward others can never be discretionary. We cannot pick and choose who or when we forgive. We cannot set up any conditions to forgive someone. I'll forgive them when _____. You fill in the blank.

If you don't get forgiveness right, everything else will be incomplete, shaky, and eventually crack.

A Better Understanding

Perspective is generally considered your fundamental outlook on life. It seems simple enough, but oh, it is anything but elementary. Your perspective becomes the way you view everything that happens to you.

But we have a troubling problem in perspective. We often look at life from our vantage point, not God's.

God's perspective is not the easiest thing to find today. The world as we know it is the enemy's territory. How do we discover God's perspective on the challenges we face? There is a simple, straightforward answer. Our perspective and truth are found in a person, and His name is Jesus. Jesus is the standard. Jesus is the prototype for forgiveness. Press into Jesus and you will discover the strength, courage, and stamina you need to live in forgiveness.

As I have traveled this challenging road of reconciliation, I have been confronted with two facets of the Christian life in which my perspective was distorted: I had stinky theology. As a result, I only partially understood the biblical dynamics of what goes into living at peace with others, not the dramatic imperative. If you don't get these two understandings correct, no matter how hard you try, you will never fully experience the biblical design of peace with others. The following two areas intersect at the epicenter of godly relationships: the fear of the Lord and suffering.

I'm guessing you are thinking, "What do the fear of God and suffering have to do with peace with others?"

The Fear of the Lord

To be obedient children of the Lord, we must have the proper mindset toward the fear of the Lord. The obvious question is, "Just what does it mean to fear the Lord?" Regrettably, I can't remember the last time I heard anyone teach about the fear of the Lord anywhere. But when we realize that the fear of the Lord is the central point in these seminal promises below, it behooves us to dig in for a better understanding of it.

- Gaining wisdom: "The fear of the LORD is the beginning of wisdom, and the knowledge of the Holy One is understanding" (Prov. 9:10).

- Having God's protection: "The angel of the LORD camps around those who fear Him, and delivers them" (Ps. 34:7, NIV).

- Attaining God's blessing: "He will bless those who fear the LORD, both the small and great ones" (Ps. 115:13).

- Extending the Lord's favor to your children: "O that there were such a heart in them that they would fear Me and always keep all My commandments, that it might be well with them and with their children forever" (Deut. 5:29).

- The necessity for a successful marriage: "Submit to one another out of reverence for Christ" (Eph. 5:21, NIV).

- Brings us life and good health: "By humility and the fear of the LORD are riches, and honor, and life" (Prov. 22:4, KJV).

- Teaches us to live in rest in this darkened world: "The fear of the Lord tends to life, and he who has it will abide satisfied; he will not be visited with evil" (Prov. 19:23, KJV).

Solomon goes as far as to say that if you seek God's wisdom, insight, and knowledge, you will eventually gain a proper understanding of the fear of the Lord.

My son, if you will receive my words, and hide my commandments within you, so that you incline your ear to wisdom, and apply your heart to understanding; yes, if you cry out for knowledge, and lift up your voice for understanding, if you seek her as silver, and search for her as for hidden treasures, then you will understand the fear of the LORD, and find the knowledge of God.

—Proverbs 2:1-5

The people of Israel stood trembling as Moses relayed God's message to them at the fringes of Mount Sinai; it included the Ten Commandments. In Exodus 20:18, thunder is booming, lightning is flashing, a trumpet is sounding, and the mountain is smoking. Wow! The people are full of fear. I would be running for cover if I had been in their sandals. They tell Moses they want nothing to do with this mighty God lest they die. Moses replies with this quizzical, seemingly contradictory response: "Do not fear, for God has come to test you, so that the fear of Him may be before you so that you do not sin" (Exod. 20:20).

Is Moses confused and sending a mixed message to the people? Which is it? Are they supposed to be afraid or not afraid?

The first use of *fear* in Exodus 20:20 is the word *yaré*.[4] It means an absolute fear to be afraid. It is the same Hebrew word used in Genesis 3:10 when Adam sinned and was scared to be found by God. When we sin and our hearts are not repentant, we may assume (wrongly) that we need to get as far away from God as possible. This is a fear that drives us away from God. Moses is instructing the people not to have this kind of fear toward God.

On the other hand, the second word for fear that Moses uses in Exodus 20:20 and wants the people to have is *yirah*.[5] It means fear, reverence, or awe, drawing us unto the Lord. And if this fear remains in us, it will help us obey and not sin. "The secret of the LORD is for those who fear Him, and

He will make them know His covenant" (Ps. 25:14, NASB). This righteous fear, *yirah*, is the same word used in Proverbs 22:4 that promises to produce life in us. "The reward of humility *and* the fear of the LORD are riches, honor, and life" (Prov. 22:4, NASB).

We don't have to look any further than Jesus to comprehend the full extent of the proper fear of the Lord and its implications for knowing God's ways. In one of the most vivid snapshots of Jesus in the Old Testament, Jesus is pictured as taking delight in the fear of the Lord. "He shall delight in the fear of the LORD, and he shall not judge by what his eyes see, nor reprove by what his ears hear" (Isa. 11:3, NASB).

The proper fear of God is the very reason Jesus could see and hear in the Spirit. Be reminded Jesus was fully man when He transcended to earth in the form of a baby to set the captives free. Because Jesus grew in stature and favor with God, righteously fearing God, He became an anathema to Satan and was bestowed full access to the counsel of God. In this state, Jesus was granted means to speak the words the Father wanted to be spoken, do the things the Father wanted done, and discern the Father's will in all matters.

A proper understanding of the fear of God will lead us to forgive others and seek forgiveness for our wrongs committed against others. It is a simple act of the will and within the grasp of any of us. My will may not be strong, but I can surrender it to God. This yielding of the will is not some extraordinary power bestowed on someone or innate within a few otherworldly saints. If, when confronted with the truth of the gospel of Jesus concerning forgiveness, we will be forgiven in the same manner we forgive others, but we still choose not to ignore or seek forgiveness, we send one of two messages to God: 1) I don't fear God, or 2) I do not believe the gospel message concerning forgiveness. Neither of these has a good ending.

A Take on Suffering

Salvation, whose cost was purchased with the greatest of all prices, the death of God's only Son, will never be gained by passive assent to the truth. We mustn't be superheroes of faith but put our faith into action. Faith isn't faith unless it acts, whether large or small. You can't have faith in a vacuum.

Confronting the brokenness in your relationships with family, past friends, church members, and others will be painful. God will never be satisfied with us living in unforgiveness toward others because it is too difficult to forgive. God will never be persuaded by our skillfully crafted statements of belief or by good works. Neither is the world or the devil fooled by such things.

There is no way around it; we also have a cross to bear.

The gospel of Jesus Christ and the gospel of the cross are at odds with our modern Christian culture. Our spiritual culture of comfort makes little room for suffering or hard things. Comfort is the American mantra. We must guard ourselves from seeing trials as coming from the devil or that God is just here to meet our needs. Following Jesus is countercultural, which plays out daily in our decisions. Howard Simon, motivational poet, penned a poem to this state.

I choose the mountain

The lowlands call
I am tempted to answer
They are offering me a free dwelling
Without having to conquer

The massive mountain makes its move
Beckoning me to ascend
A much more difficult path
To get up the slippery bend

I cannot choose both
I have a choice to make
I must be wise
This will determine my fate

I choose, I choose the mountain
With all its stress and strain
Because only by climbing
Can I rise above the plain

I choose the mountain
And I will never stop climbing
I choose the mountain
And I shall forever be ascending[6]

To put it bluntly, the correct theology about suffering means I must decide to let the other person off the hook for the pain they are responsible for in my life—what a courageous and difficult decision. This is choosing the mountain, the arduous undertaking that St. Paul speaks of to the Philippians: "Therefore, my beloved, as you have always obeyed, not only in my presence but so much more in my absence, work out your own salvation with fear and trembling" (Phil. 2:12, KJV).

Living in forgiveness with others is offering our bodies as a living sacrifice. Forgiving others for their sin and seeking forgiveness for our wrongdoings crucifies our flesh and the pride that typifies our Adamic motivations. It is participating in Christ's sufferings in a tangible, irrefutable manner. This is the crucible of transformation—where the precious gold is purified.

Therefore if you have any encouragement from being united with Christ, if any comfort from his love, if any common sharing in the Spirit, if any tenderness and compassion, then make my joy complete by being like-minded, having the same love, being one in spirit and of one mind. Do nothing out of selfish ambition or vain conceit. Rather, in humility value others above yourselves, not looking to your own interests but each of you to the interests of the others. In your relationships with one another, have the same mindset as Christ Jesus: Who, being in very nature God, did not consider equality with God something to be used to his own advantage; rather, he made himself nothing by taking the very nature of a servant, being made in human likeness. And being found in appearance as a man, he humbled himself by becoming obedient to death—even death on a cross!

—Philippians 2:1-8, NIV

Here, comfortable Christianity gets painful.

- As we yearn for the love of God to flow from us, we are paired with the downcast.

- We pray for Jesus' love to act through us and are called to serve those we have no natural affinity for.

- We answer the call to forgive those who have harmed us and seek forgiveness from those we have hurt.

When we get our theology right about forgiveness and do not balk or allow ourselves to be repulsed at its suffering and cost, we will touch the brotherly love God intended all along. "As concerning brotherly love, you do not need me to write to you. For you yourselves are taught by God to love one another. And indeed, you do have love for all the brothers in Macedonia. But we urge you, brothers, that you increase more and more" (1 Thess. 4:9-10).

Through the mercy of God, we learn to accept one another as Christ has accepted us. Because we are the objects of Christ's unsearchable abyss of peace, He provides the power for us to conquer anything that would quell our brotherly love. "Therefore, accept one another, just as Christ also accepted us, for the glory of God" (Rom. 15:7, NASB). We now know that the forgiveness we offer and seek from others is a shadow of the mountain of forgiveness Christ purchased for our redemption.

A Better, More Straightforward Theology

Division $\rightarrow$ Peace $\rightarrow$ Encouraging one another

The Christians in Paul's day in Rome lived chaotic lives. Paul wrote the letter to the Romans to persuade them to build peaceful and deep relationships in all the house churches despite everything around them.

Paul does a beautiful thing in the last three chapters of Romans. He gives them instructions on how to live with different opinions without squabbling. Paul teaches the Romans that each person can follow the Spirit's impressions, though they may be different from others, and maintain unity. He guides them into understanding that "non-essentials" exist in life, even some that may have spiritual implications. Paul introduces a majestic thought: Sometimes, we must lay down our fondness for certain things for love and peace. He repeatedly addresses this theme of peace between Christians in the body in these closing chapters of Romans.

Paul's theme is timeless.

"But as for you, why do you judge your brother or sister?" (Rom. 14:10a, NASB).

"Now may the God who gives perseverance and encouragement grant you to be of the same mind with one another according to Jesus Christ" (Rom. 15:5, NASB).

"Wherefore, accept one another, just as Christ also accepted us to the glory of God" (Rom. 15:7, NASB).

"Now I urge you, brethren, keep your eye on those who cause dissensions and hindrances contrary to the teaching which you learned, and turn away from them" (Rom. 16:17, NASB).

Paul's instruction is pointed: Don't allow division and pursue peace. But he takes it to the majestic pinnacle, Christ's inevitable destination: Build each other up—encouragement.

"So then let us pursue the things which make for peace and the building up of one another" (Rom. 14:19, NASB).

"And concerning you, my brothers *and sisters*, I myself also am convinced that you yourselves are full of goodness, filled with all knowledge and able also to admonish one another" (Rom. 15:14, NASB).

Take a Test Drive with the Correct Theology

Ask the Holy Spirit to bring anyone you are separated from to your mind. It could be an offense you have taken or one someone has with you. Is there anyone you need to forgive or know is holding ill feelings and unforgiveness toward you?

Pause here and wait sixty seconds; time yourself.

You are the dramatic exception if the Holy Spirit does not bring a person or an issue to your remembrance. Do write down the name(s) the Spirit just brought to your mind.

You may discover that other people will come to your attention as you read this book. Write these people's names down in your journal. If you don't have a spiritual journal, start one; this step alone could be the most profound thing this book may bring you. Please heed this advice: If you are like most people and me, when you don't write down things the Spirit of God has revealed, they will be lost forever.

Don't get ahead of yourself and run out trying to resolve these broken relationships the Spirit has made you aware of. Remember the name(s), though. Finish this book and then get to work on your relationships.

Spiritual reality butts into our lives when we confront unforgiveness and separation from others. God is in the process of transforming us through the Holy Spirit. For most of us, if not all, this means having God dig up some of the foundations of our theology (beliefs) and getting it right.

Be bold and allow the Holy Spirit to illuminate your beliefs about forgiveness, the fear of God, and suffering.

CHAPTER 5

NOW OPEN YOUR BOSOM TO THE WIND'S FREE PLAY

Nevertheless I tell you the truth; it is expedient for you that I go away: for if I go not away, the Comforter will not come unto you; but if I depart, I will send him unto you. And when he is come, he will reprove the world of sin, and of righteousness, and of judgment.

—John 16:7-8

Scores of books have been written about the Holy Spirit. My chapter snippet is a snapshot of but one facet: The Spirit is crucial in fostering forgiveness in relationships and reconciliation.

The most staggering and vital consideration of the Spirit is this irrefutable admission: The Holy Spirit is as much God as God the Father and Jesus the Son. "Now the Lord is the Spirit..." (2 Cor. 3:17). And in Acts, Luke recorded what Peter told Ananias after he pointed out Ananias had lied to the Holy Spirit: Peter added the addendum, "You did not lie to men, but to God" (Acts 5:4b).

In Deuteronomy 6:4-6 we find the Shema, which most religious Jews pray twice daily. It is familiar to most Christians as well. Jesus even quoted this scripture twice. "Hear, O Israel: The LORD is our God. The LORD is one! And you shall love the LORD your God with all your heart and with all your soul and with all your might. These words, which I am commanding you today, shall be in your heart." There is one God, and the word used here is *e·ḥād*, meaning a singular God;[1] it is the same word used in Genesis 2:24 to describe Adam and Eve becoming one flesh. The Holy Spirit is one with God. I don't believe the Book of Deuteronomy receives its appropriate homage; it is a crucial book written to educate and inspire the children of Israel to understand God wants obedience in both thoughts and actions. Obedience to the Word of God is a principle consideration in this quest for forgiveness.

Jesus Christ came into the world for one primary reason: to take away the sins of the world and, in so doing, reconcile men and women to God and each other. The Holy Spirit is God and works with God to bring about God's purposes. I will say it repeatedly until you can invariably sense it coming: *God's essential purpose is unity.* He wants us reconciled to each other. The Holy Spirit is the spirit of fellowship.

Our modern American denominations have a real problem with the Holy Spirit. Many denominations simply don't believe what Scripture teaches about the Holy Spirit, and so many Christians do not know the Holy Spirit as a person. How well do you know the Holy Spirit? It is a weighty question, and most Christians don't understand how to get to know the Holy Spirit.

How Do You Get to Know Someone?

It is the penetrating question you must answer to access the Holy Spirit's power for your life and relationships: How do you get to know someone? If you have ever been in love, one of the first things you notice is that you want to be with the other person all the time. Do a quick stop and recall your first love, the tenderness, and all the time you spent with the other person. Do you remember that touch? The distinct smell? The love you had for just talking and talking and talking?

Time is the most critical factor in getting to know someone. And if you want to know someone fully, ask them penetrating questions and just listen. You do not get to know someone by talking about yourself. You must spend quality time listening to the Holy Spirit to understand the nuances of His personality. Again, He is a person.

A few years back, I spent approximately two years in the throes of physical failure (two total knee replacements, a repeat third knee replacement, and back surgeries). During this period, I studied all the times Jesus prayed in the Scriptures. After exhaustive research and reading the New Testament over and over, I identified twenty-three times when Jesus prayed. My goal was to find out what Jesus' prayer life was like. What themes and constants emerged from the times Jesus prayed to the Father? How could Jesus know the Father's will so clearly that He only spoke what the Father wanted spoken and only did the Father's will?

After months of meditating on the prayers of Jesus, the critical factor of Jesus' prayer life became glaring to me with cast-iron certainty. During Jesus' prayer time, He spent much more time listening to God the Father than talking to Him. In Isaiah 50, we have a marvelous still shot of Jesus that confirms that Jesus listened intently to the Father much more than He talked to Him. "The LORD God has given Me the tongue of disciples, so that I may know how to sustain the weary one with a word. He awakens *Me* morning by morning, He awakens My ear to listen as a disciple" (Isa. 50:4, NASB). This is the picture of Jesus listening to the Father every morning as if He were the Father's disciple.

My wife, Annamae, has more godly wisdom than anyone I know. As we have served as elders in a body of Christ in our city, it has become apparent that I'm not the only one in our elder group who acknowledges her spiritual acuity. One of our pastors recently remarked, "When Annamae says something, we should just save time and do it." He was being facetious, but we all knew the point he wanted to make. Annamae is quick to discern the will of the Lord in issues we face as elders, and we need to listen to her.

There is another exceptional feature about my wife. She has a cadre of women who call her their best friend. Most of these women are mature, seasoned Christians. As I have observed my wife's friendships, I've seen two remarkable features: 1) Annamae is rarely in a hurry with people; when she engages, she engages fully. As a sidebar to this, there is another critical element: She is rarely the person who ends conversations with her friends. 2) Annamae knows her friends. She has often told me you must listen and understand your friends if you want deep-hearted, intimate friendships. Here is where I am heading with this tale of my wife. She is a friend of the Holy Spirit. She has an intimate, firsthand understanding of what pleases the Holy Spirit and does those things.

You need to know the Holy Spirit as a friend, His gradations and what pleases and displeases Him. The Holy Spirit must have our time and attention. Author Dr. Greg Cole is on to something when he says, "The ones we linger with are the ones we grow to love. There is no deep belonging without lingering."[2]

The Holy Spirit leads us into all truth (John 16:13). The fact is that God has called us to live in forgiveness toward one another and reconcile with any Christians from whom we are estranged. This great truth can only come to fruition through the work of the Holy Spirit and His power in us: The degree to which I submit my life to the Holy Spirit, inviting Him into my life unconditionally and coming to know Him deeply, is the degree to which I will be able to live in forgiveness toward others.

I say then, walk in the Spirit, and you shall not fulfill the lust of the flesh. Now the works of the flesh are revealed, which are these:

Adultery, sexual immorality, impurity, lewdness, idolatry, sorcery, hatred, strife, jealousy, rage, selfishness, dissensions, heresies, envy, murders, drunkenness, carousing, and the like. I warn you, as I previously warned you, that those who do such things shall not inherit the kingdom of God.

—Galatians 5:16, 19-21

Hatred, jealousy, rage, selfishness, dissension, and so on are the sins of the flesh that destroy fellowship in Christ. It isn't as if the Word of God doesn't teach us how to live with each other. But it is only in the power of the Holy Spirit that Christ's essential purpose will manifest in our midst (Acts 1:8). Paul instructs us explicitly how to interact with other Christians; it includes none of the unity busters at the beginning of this paragraph. Instead, Paul says, "But be filled with the Spirit. Speak to one another in psalms, hymns, and spiritual songs, singing and making melody in your heart to the Lord" (Eph. 5:18b-19).

Sadly, everyone knows Christian after Christian who exhibits little self-control when it comes to the issues with our tongue—perhaps we are that person time and again (more on this to come in chapter 8.)

We desperately need the Holy Spirit to touch us again and put a new song in our mouths. We must have the Spirit of God operating in our life. Only by His power can we overcome these sins of the flesh that are detrimental to fellowship with others. And we must be zealous to seek the Spirit's fresh infilling daily. In Ephesians 5:18 above, the phrase "be filled" connotes a continual filling of the Spirit that keeps us full to our capacity.[3] I often say this to my friends, and if you asked any of them what is foremost on my heart these days, they would say, "Tim is desperate for the discernment and power of the Holy Spirit in his life."

George MacDonald, Scottish author, Christian minister, and pioneering figure in modern fantasy literature, penned this verse, which aptly describes the zeal we must display after the Spirit, giving Him free rein in our lives and opening our inner man to the Spirit's free play.

But he who would be born again indeed,
Must wake his soul unnumbered times a day,
And urge himself to life with holy greed;
Now ope his bosom to the Wind's free play;
And now, with patience forceful, hard, lie still,
Submiss and ready to the making will,
Athirst and empty, for God's breath to fill.[4]

We must allow the Holy Spirit to reign freely in our lives. Complete forgiveness and reconciliation with those separated can become a divine reality. There is one position for a greater anointing of the Spirit: "Submiss and ready to the making will."

And what about that power?

The Holy Spirit will lead us into all truth. And here is the truth: We have no innate power to live the Christian life. If I think I can muster up the strength to live at peace with all men and women alone, I don't need the enemy to deceive me; I have deceived myself. When Paul begins his famous portrayal of the Christian's armor to use to battle the enemy, Satan, he starts at the beginning and concludes in the same place. There is only one ground to stand on: the strength of the Lord. "Finally, my brothers, be strong in the Lord and in the power of His might" (Eph. 6:10).

The power we have to apply to healing our relationships is the same power that raised Christ from the dead. The power of the Holy Spirit is perfect and just what we need. Paul precedes his preamble on the armor of God (Eph. 6:10-18) by praying that we won't be hard-headed and instead be teachable to have faith in God's strength at work in our lives (Eph. 1:17-20). And for those like myself (in need of reteaching), Paul prays to the Father that we would be strengthened by the Spirit (Eph. 3:16-17).

Take the time to read Isaiah 11:2-3; you will be greatly encouraged. In this snapshot of Jesus, we read the seven attributes of the Holy Spirit of God that will rest on Him (two of which are counsel and strength). These seven Spirits of God are referenced again in Revelation 1:4, 3:1, 4:5, and 5:6. Can you use some counsel and strength of the Holy Spirit in your life today as you navigate family, friendships, and associations? Be convinced today, fellow followers of Christ, that His divine power is working in us and will, by faith, be manifest in our relationships. We have the power!

The Dove

The following question is among the most important you will grapple with in your Christian life. And I believe the answer is as startling as it is discomforting.

What is the primary culprit that derails God's intentions for unity in the body of Christ—a unity that would enthrall nonbelievers to consider Jesus Christ as Savior?

Let me propose this answer.

We grieve the One who is the instigator, facilitator, and giver of the capacity for Christians to live in intimacy and unity—the Holy Spirit. There is a fellowship between believers that can only be grasped with the Holy Spirit of God in operation and control.

What does it mean to grieve the Holy Spirit? The answer is straightforward, but to appreciate it fully, we must first pinpoint some of the characteristics of this person, the Holy Spirit. The dove is identified as a symbol of the Holy Spirit in the Scriptures. All four Gospel accounts of Jesus' baptism identify the Holy Spirit coming as a dove and descending on Jesus.

"Doves are often seen as symbols of peace, spirituality, hope, renewal, transformation, and love," explains Johanna Aúgusta."[5] Another writer says the traits of a dove are soft and calming and rarely seem rushed. He says that while doves are shy and friendly, they lead in their own way. They are builders of peace and harmony; they are peacekeepers.[6]

These terms, shy, calming, friendly, and peacekeepers, portray the Holy Spirit's temperament. And I propose they are best totted up in one word: *sensitivity.*

We often hear and use this phrase when discussing the Holy Spirit: the sensitivity of the Spirit. If you have any connection to the Holy Spirit, you intuitively recognize this characteristic of the Holy Spirit. I am leaning on *Merriam-Webster* for a definition. Sensitive: 1) easily hurt or damaged, 2) delicately aware of the attitudes and feelings of others.[7]

The Holy Spirit is easily grieved. And He is primarily grieved by the way we treat each other. He is not just sensitive; He is super sensitive. This may be the most sobering lesson I have learned in the last twenty years: The Holy Spirit grieves easily, and His sensitivity quickly leaves me when I grieve Him. Let's be clear; I am not saying I lose the Holy Spirit in my life. No. He has taken up residence in me, and I am His temple. But when I grieve Him, I lose the sensitivity I must have to recognize the enemy's schemes to disrupt my relationships and create division. I forfeit the Holy Spirit's power. Only through His power can I overcome the world, the flesh, and the devil, which are all about destroying the unity of God's children.

In Jesus' well-known, expansive passage (Matt. 10:1-42), in which He is instructing the disciples before sending them out on their own for a trial run at the ministry, He says, "Behold, I am sending you out as sheep in the midst of wolves; so be as wary as serpents, and as innocent as doves (Matt. 10:16, NASB). The *Merriam-Webster* dictionary, which has been around since 1828, defines innocence as free from guilt or sin, especially through lack of knowledge of evil.[8]

A friend and I were discussing the enemy's myriad schemes to create division in our lives: offense, misunderstandings, family issues, judging others; the list goes on unceremoniously. My friend, who has a banking background, shared a story he heard that helped us understand the most practical way to be on our spiritual guard. He recalled how treasury agents and bankers are trained to identify counterfeit money. He said they teach bankers to recognize counterfeits by training them to identify the bona fide bills. The bankers and agents don't focus on studying counterfeit bills. They arduously study the authentic bills, which trains their brain to recognize the forgeries quickly and accurately. One writer went as far as to say, "They do not bother to handle counterfeits, but real money—lots of real money."[9]

As a school headmaster, I walked into a middle school room and noticed a small group of girls looking at skimpy bathing suits on a computer. They didn't see me walk up and paid no attention to the sixth-grade boy sitting by them either. As I walked up, I noticed the boy slightly glanced at what the girls were absorbing. His immediate response was captivating. He turned his head away instantly, and in a manner that encapsulated pure innocence and embarrassment. Yes, here is the big deal.

Hang out with the Holy Spirit and you will learn how to have sweet fellowship with others and quickly identify the enemy's schemes intended to derail friendship, fellowship, and unity.

The Most Crucial Chapter in the New Testament (Outside the Gospels)

I hold that Ephesians 4 is the most vital chapter in the New Testament outside those in the Gospels. The NIV rightly titles this chapter "Unity and Maturity in the Body of Christ."[10]

Paul begins this exposé encouraging Christians to walk worthy of their calling by having humility, gentleness, patience, and forbearance to one another in love (Eph. 4:1-2). Then Paul pinpoints the preeminent thought of the chapter, that we are to be diligent to preserve the unity of the Spirit (Eph. 4:3). This is the Father, Son, and Holy Spirit's plan that will draw people into the church; there is no fallback strategy, no plan B.

God proposes that this unity will be so enticing to those in the world that they must have and be a part of it. We must be diligent in maintaining this unity.

To make sure there is no misunderstanding about this unity, Paul describes in detail what is offered to Gentiles and Jews alike. There is one body, one Spirit, one hope, one Lord, one faith, one baptism, one God and Father who is over all (Eph. 4-6). There is no room for division in the body of Christ; love and forgiveness must reign.

I believe Ephesians 4:11-16 is the most precise statement in the New Testament describing the purpose of the church. Everything that takes place in the Christian life equips us to build up the body (the church) to attain the unity of the faith in the fullness of Christ. Everyone plays a part in this maturing, transforming aspiration; it is a team sport. It may necessitate speaking the truth to one another, but all things are done in love. Let me be redundant for clarity; no one gets a free pass because of offense, hurt, unforgiveness, likes or dislikes, bias, or any other cause. We all are strategic and needed for the body of Christ to mature. We cannot fulfill our calling and role if we hold on to unforgiveness or refuse to offer forgiveness to others.

> So Christ himself gave the apostles, the prophets, the evangelists, the pastors and teachers, to equip his people for works of service, so that the body of Christ may be built up until we all reach unity in the faith and in the knowledge of the Son of God and become mature, attaining to the whole measure of the fullness of Christ. Then we will no longer be infants, tossed back and forth by the waves, and blown here and there by every wind of teaching and by the cunning and craftiness of people in their deceitful scheming. Instead, speaking the truth in love, we will grow to become in every respect the mature body of him who is the head, that is, Christ. From him the whole body, joined and held together by

every supporting ligament, grows and builds itself up in love, as each part does its work.

—Ephesians 4:11-16, NIV

What follows in the rest of the fourth chapter of Ephesians is the zenith in understanding what creates and destroys unity.

What produces unity:

- "be made new in the attitude of your minds" v. 3
- "put on the new self, created in the likeness of God" v. 24
- "Do not let the sun go down while you are still angry" v. 26
- "and do not give the devil a foothold" v. 27

Paul identifies how we grieve the Holy Spirit (vv. 25-31). He sandwiches these actions that grieve the Holy Spirit around a seminal injunction with outstanding clarity and intent in verse 30, "Do not grieve the Holy Spirit of God, by whom you were sealed for the day of redemption" (Eph. 4:30, NASB).

This is Paul's litany of deeds that grieve the Holy Spirit and obliterate unity:

Actions before verse 30, verses 25-29

- Falsehoods
- Being angry and sinning (it is OK to get mad; just don't sin)
- Unwholesome words
- Stealing

Actions following verse 30, verse 31

- Bitterness
- Wrath and anger
- Clamor (loud shouting)
- Slander
- Malice

What is the common denominator in these actions that grieve the Holy Spirit? It is the way we treat one another. Our sins grieve the Holy Spirit and will permanently block our potential to have the Spirit in complete operation in our lives (His sensitivity.) These unwholesome actions and words give way to situations that require forgiveness and reconciliation for the body to be healthy and whole.

The Holy Spirit of God is the great agent of holiness and unity. We don't see Him, but He is there, ever-present, patient, waiting on us to submit our lives. The Holy Spirit cries out today for you to allow Him to search your heart for unforgiveness. What offenses lie in your heart?

"The Spirit brings order out of chaos and beauty out of ugliness. He can transform a sin-blistered man into a paragon of virtue. The Spirit changes people. The author of life is also the Transformer of life."[11] —R. C. Sproul

Christian, will you open your bosom to the wind's free play?

CHAPTER 6

WHY SO LITTLE OF THE KINGDOM OF HEAVEN?

But He said to them, "I must also preach the kingdom of God to the other cities, because I was sent for this *purpose*."

—Luke 4:43, NASB

If we can understand the kingdom of heaven, we will realize the spiritual devastation that severed relationships produce in God's eternal purpose—unity. Let's get this correct as we begin: The kingdom of heaven is a mystery; sometimes I muse whether God glories in the mysteriousness of it all. Only the Holy Spirit can reveal the kingdom to a person. We are human and see in part, but there is a greater mystery. God, by His Holy Spirit, makes all things known to us, even giving us the mind of Christ (1 Cor. 9-16). Wow!

Christ's mission on earth depends upon the kingdom of heaven revealed in our midst. That mission finds its expression in the unity of believers. That's a big project. Yes, but it has no chance of fruition unless we know what the kingdom of heaven is, where it is, and what part we play in its fulfillment. But the fact is, most of us don't know what the kingdom of heaven is, don't know how to find it, and have little idea what we are looking for. And to be as pointed as I can muster, if we can't get along with each other, we have only a little hope of ever experiencing the kingdom of heaven. That's the gist of it—game over. We must grasp this understanding: If we can't live in forgiveness and contend for reconciliation, not only will we be oblivious to the kingdom of God, but we will never be able to recognize it.

The Kingdom of Heaven

What do you think was the core of Jesus' teaching and preaching? You've got it, the "kingdom of God." It is mentioned fifty-three times in the New Testament, and the "kingdom of heaven" appears thirty-two times. Jesus speaks of the kingdom of God often with crowds and the disciples. He says the kingdom of heaven is like a mustard seed, a treasure, the merchant trying to find fine pearls, or the king who gives a banquet. Jesus even goes as far as to use the kingdom to identify His mission on earth (Luke 4:43, above).

And if you need more convincing on the importance of the kingdom, consider this: After Jesus was raised from the dead and had His last face-to-face encounters with the disciples, what did He do with them? Jesus spent forty days teaching them about the kingdom of God. "After his suffering, he presented himself to them and gave many convincing proofs that he was alive. He appeared to them for forty days and spoke about the kingdom of God" (Acts 1:3, NIV). And it wasn't just Jesus who placed such an emphasis on the kingdom. Luke summated everything Paul taught in his years in Rome: "He proclaimed the kingdom of God and taught about the Lord Jesus Christ—with all boldness and without hindrance!" (Acts 31:28, NIV).

Most Christians are everything from mystified to befuddled about the kingdom of God or heaven. Many denominations believe it is the church. "Since the days of Augustine, the Kingdom of Heaven has been identified with the Church."[1] Some believe the kingdom of God is where social justice has finally arrived, brought on by all-encompassing positive changes in social order and laws. Things like discrimination, prejudice, and poverty will all change due to the influence of God (with a lot of help from us). And it is vogue today to dwindle the kingdom of God to an inner experience like the monks of old had with spiritual guides, spiritual formation coaches, and spiritual gurus.

I must confess one predisposition: I don't believe the church is the kingdom of heaven. You don't need heavenly discernment to survey the state of most churches and conclude, nope, certainly not what God intended.

How does a little, staggering verse like the following float by us and nonchalantly end up banked away in our favorite portfolio of Scripture memory or on a Christian bookmark? "But seek first the kingdom of God and His righteousness, and all these things shall be given to you" (Matt. 6:33). Are we spiritually blind (Matt. 13:14-15)? It seems there should be more than just a smidgen of alarm that we have not come to grips with the kingdom of heaven. It must be an object of our travail, not social justice, not the church, nor heaven itself.

For most of my Christian life, I believed that the kingdom was an internal, idiosyncratic experience—there's that foundational belief system again from chapter 4. If I could practice Christian disciplines thoroughly enough, I would be mystically transformed and experience the kingdom of God in my heart. Voilà! Righteous man of God.

The Culture of the Kingdom

"No one has seen God at any time. If we love one another, God dwells in us, and His love is perfected in us" (1 John 4:12).

"We love Him because He first loved us. If anyone says, 'I love God,' and hates his brother, he is a liar. For whoever does not love his brother whom he has seen, how can he love God whom he has not seen?" (1 John 4:19-20).

The kingdom of God has a culture, and it is love. Love is everything. Love is the vision of the kingdom and what the kingdom is all about. Because this vision is so elementary, it can become cliché at times. I hear people use the word *love*, which often comes across as trite and trivial—it is anything but that. Love is bold, radical, and breathtaking. It leaves me wondering if we are speaking the same language. And the mic drops as John delivers this verse, "We have this commandment from Him: Whoever loves God must also love his brother" (1 John 4:21). John lets all readers know for eternity that we have this commandment directly from Jesus: Whoever loves God must love his brother. Why do we have so little of the kingdom of heaven? We have many people refusing to forgive and love their brother or sister.

I can think of no more straightforward explanation of what God is up to in the life of the believer in the world than to say: God, through the Holy Spirit, is spreading His love abroad in our hearts for the sake of the world.

In the most well-known expose and coda ever written on love (1 Corinthians 13), Paul concludes by saying three things remain: faith, hope, and love, and the greatest of these is love (1 Cor. 13:13). The most supreme thing God can ever accomplish in the life of a believer is the love of Christ. Paul is shockingly clear; no Christian attribute or gift can match love.

The Sadducees were conspiring one day to trap Jesus but failed (Matthew 22). Next up were the Pharisees. They all huddled and came up with their question—sure to stump Jesus—and wouldn't you know it, they sent an attorney to question Him! He asks, "Teacher, which is the greatest commandment in the law?" (Matt. 22:36). The Pharisees just don't get who they are addressing. In one fell swoop, Jesus sums up the Law (and there were many laws) and the Prophets, the Torah, and the entire Old Testament in these same commandments. Stunning!

"Jesus said to him, 'You shall love the Lord your God with all your heart, and with all your soul, and with all your mind. This is the first and great commandment. And the second is like it: 'You shall love your neighbor as yourself.' On these two commandments hang all the Law and the Prophets" (Matt. 22:37-40).

What do we think when we refuse to forgive others and seek forgiveness for our offenses against others? Do we really believe we can experience the fullness of the kingdom of heaven in our midst?

The success of God's kingdom on earth depends on the unity of the church—the unity of individual believers. If we think we can work for God and not pay attention to the broken relationships in our lives, we are deceived and have chosen to settle for less. Disunity affects the value of our work for Christ. Settling to exist in brokenness with our family, friends (former friends), and others in the body of Christ and continuing to work diligently for Christ is to be seduced by the good. The good is always the enemy of the best.

But praise God—He has given us the Holy Spirit to enable us to love each other. Paul states it perfectly and directly. "And hope does not put us to shame, because God's love has been poured out in our hearts through the Holy Spirit, who has been given to us" (Rom. 5:5, NIV).

There are two dramatic and crucial understandings to be gained by Paul's teaching in Romans 5:5: 1) We will never be able to muster the strength to love God or others on our own; that's the truth, plain and simple. 2) We have the Holy Spirit within us, and He is ever entreating us to yield more of our hearts to Him.

The love of Jesus is the foundation of our salvation, but not just that. His love is the impetus for our daily living and behavior toward others.

When you get up in the morning and dress, love is your most essential clothing. God has chosen us to be holy as He is holy. We must decide daily to give a margin for others' faults and offenses. Loving God's people will likely mean disappointment, heartache, and offense. The only way to not be hurt is not to love. What a shallow, sad way of living.

"Since God chose you to be the holy people he loves, you must clothe yourselves with tenderhearted mercy, kindness, humility, gentleness, and patience. Make allowance for each other's faults and forgive anyone who offends you. Remember, the Lord forgave you, so you must forgive others. Above all, clothe yourselves with love, which binds us all together in perfect harmony" (Col. 3:12-14, NLT).

With the great unrest in our country today, the political tension, the racial hatred, confusion, and loathing toward those with different sexual orientations, and division among Christians, we are desperate for the love of God to be working in the hearts of men and women. The love of God's kingdom is needed in Satan's kingdom of the world.

Experiencing the Kingdom

I have always believed we come to know and experience the kingdom of heaven in three distinct ways: our personal experience (inwardly fueled by intimacy with Jesus), the Word, and our interaction with the world community (putting our faith in Christ into action). In these areas, we confront lies, strongholds, and the enemy, all of which rebuff Christ's essential purpose, oneness with the Trinity and oneness with others.

Experiencing the Kingdom Through Our Personal Experience

Everything in the Christian life begins with intimacy with Jesus. This intimacy results from an abiding relationship with Christ through prayer, fasting, giving, and other spiritual disciplines. But we must get this straight: Spiritual disciplines exist for this and this reason only—intimacy with Jesus. We are missing the whole point if spirituality is relegated to spiritual disciplines and their performance. And we have created an alternative gospel called dead religion! Spiritual disciplines are subservient to the kingdom.

If the Holy Spirit is not entirely relied upon, spiritual disciplines will produce self-righteousness, legalism, and judgmentalism. The kingdom of heaven is subject to the ministry of the Holy Spirit. It is not subject to the spiritual supermen or superwomen we wrongly assume we become when mastering one of the spiritual disciplines—for example, we become good at fasting. A missionary friend, Ken Griffin, recently told me, "God does not command me to engage in these 'disciplines.' I do them because I want to have a personal encounter with God. If I were engaged in these activities for any other reason than love, I would question my motives for doing so."

The greatest trap is thinking we must earn intimacy with Jesus through discipline or jump through some spiritual hoop to receive God's blessing. I love the spiritual disciplines, but here's the truth: The food that Jesus offers each of us is free. Come and eat your fill!

Richard Foster's marvelous book *Celebration of Discipline* identifies twelve spiritual disciplines.[2] Regardless of the conjecture concerning how many spiritual disciplines there are, when you peruse various lists, you will almost always see prayer, the study of the Word, fasting, service to others, and various aspects of community life.

You will have personal, daily repentance where you have the Spirit of the Lord and intimacy with Jesus. True, godly repentance will always bring a person to consider the divisions and separations in their life. The doors to the kingdom come flying open when a person faces the pain of repentance. My wife, Annamae, has it right: "Daily repentance takes you higher up in the Lord. Accumulating more knowledge, information, truth, or understanding will take you nowhere." I'll add my addendum to her quote:

More and more knowledge will gain you the applause of man and sorrow (Eccles. 1:18).

The demands of the kingdom of heaven point to one position in life: childlikeness. When we perfectly relate to Jesus, it is through the actual life of a child, simple and free from self-consciousness.

I took my granddaughter and grandson canoeing this past fall. JJ, who was six then, is friendly and seeks out other children to play with wherever he goes. The lake we went to that day was strangely void of other people, except one father and daughter of a different race than JJ. The two of them were obviously not veteran lake-goers. In only minutes, JJ had approached the little girl his age, and they were off, wholeheartedly playing like mad, laughing, screeching, and splashing at the water's edge. I'm an ardent canoe aficionado—having taught canoeing in Red Cross summer camps—so I eventually talked the dad into letting the little girl take her first ride in a canoe (of course, wearing a lifejacket) with me. Oh, and the waters were as calm as a baby deep asleep by her mother's side. This is what little and grown-up children do and see. They accept others. Race or color is not an issue.

We must return to childlike faith and actions to unite our relationships. We choose to believe the Scriptures at face value. "Whatever happens, conduct yourselves in a manner worthy of the gospel of Christ. Then, whether I come and see you or only hear about you in my absence, I will know that you stand firm in the *one* Spirit, striving together as *one* for the faith of the gospel" (Phil. 1:27, NIV).

What if God's purpose for us is to grow and be "deformed" into the image of a child? How does that compare to the continual accumulation of spiritual knowledge, sophistication of life, and honing of our ever-expanding giftedness?

Experiencing the Kingdom Through the Word

The Word reveals God.
In the Word, God answers us.
In the Word, God comes to dwell with us.
In the Word, God gives Himself to us.[3]

The Word of God is indispensable in experiencing intimacy with God and the kingdom. In speaking of the Word in Proverbs, Solomon said, "When you go, they will lead you; when you sleep, they will keep you; and when you awake, they will speak with you" (Prov. 6:22). Thank God for His Word!

The Word of God is our guide to reconciliation with others. You have seen in this book scripture after scripture concerning God's instruction, goal, and heart for our harmony. Reconciliation is the consistent theme in God's Word from Genesis to Revelation, our reconciliation with God and each other. It simply cannot be ignored.

It is vital in reading a book to know its plot. The plot of the Bible is simple: God wants a family and a bride for His Son. We are that bride Christ is patiently waiting for, and He is looking for the allure of our love for Him and one another.

If you are hungry for the presence of God in your life, just develop a taste for God's Word. I have a confession on this thought, and it is not a boast. I am addicted to the Word of God. I've traded in my worldly obsessions for this one. I hunger and thirst for the Word of God every morning when I wake. It is my food first thing in the morning when I awake in bed through prayers and scriptures I have hidden in my heart, and when I get out of bed, I partake of the Word in quiet, waiting before the Lord in prayer before I do anything else for the day.

Have you experienced this trade that an unknown author penned in this lovely poem?

Fearing to launch on "full surrender's" tide,
I asked the Lord where would its waters glide
My little bark, "To troubled seas I dread?"
"Unto Myself," He said.

Weeping beside an open grave I stood,
In bitterness of soul I cried to God:
"Where leads this path of sorrow that I tread?"
"Unto Myself," He said.

Striving for souls, I loved the work too well;
Then disappointments came; I could not tell
The reason, till He said, "I am think all;
Unto Myself I call."

Watching my heroes—those I love the best—
I saw them fail; they could not stand the test,
Even by this the Lord, through tears not few,
Unto Himself me drew.

Unto Himself! Nor earthly tongue can tell
The bliss I find, since in His heart I swell;
The things that charmed me once seem all as naught;
Unto Himself I'm brought.[4]

Have you developed a taste for the Word of God? There is an imagery seen repeatedly in Scripture of consuming God's Word. In Job 23:12, Job said to one of his friends, "I have not failed the commands of His lips; I have treasured the words of His mouth more than my necessary food" (NASB). We are not sure who wrote Psalm 119, but his proclamation was clear concerning the words of God, "How sweet are Your words to the taste of my mouth! Sweeter than honey to my mouth!" (Ps. 119:103). And

Jesus spoke it clearly in the Sermon on the Mount when He said, "Blessed are those who hunger and thirst for righteousness, for they shall be filled" (Matt. 5:6).

When you develop an insatiable hunger for the Word of God, your mind transforms and changes your thoughts. The outcome is predictable. You will become hungry for the food Jesus hungered for: to do His Father's will (John 4:34).

Few issues are less debatable in the kingdom of heaven than God's will concerning His followers: that they would be one.

Are you hungry? The hungry will always get fed.

Experiencing the Kingdom Through the World and Community with the Saints

Our interaction with the world and each other is where we put our faith into action. Christ has called us to be His ambassadors to a dying and hurting world (2 Cor. 5:20). Jesus made it clear in His High Priestly prayer of John 17 that this is our calling into the world. And He continually identifies the need for our oneness with Him and each other, the things that will keep us safe from the world's influence on us and the church.

"I am to be no longer in the world, **though these are in the world**, for I am coming to You. Holy Father, through Your name keep those whom You have given Me, **that they may be one as We are one**" (John 17:11).

"I have given them Your word. And the world has hated them because **they are not of the world**, just as I am not of the world" (John 17:14).

"**I do not pray that You should take them out of the world**, but that You should keep them from the evil one" (John 17:15).

"**They are not of the world** even as I am not of the world" (John 17:16).

"That they may all be one, as You, Father, are in Me, and I in You. May they also be one in Us, that the world may believe that You have sent Me" (John 17:21).

"I have declared Your name to them, and will declare it, **that the love with which You loved Me may be in them, and I in them"** (John 17:26).

To discern the kingdom of God, we must face this truth: The world belongs to Satan. On the other hand, we are not citizens of Satan's realm (Phil. 3:20-21; 2 Cor. 4:4).

The spirits of this evil age are the lust of the flesh, the lust of the eyes, and the pride of life. The enemy has blinded and deceived many Christians into believing that friendship with the world is not a sin. This friendship with the world bleeds into the heart subtly and shrewdly. When we love the things of the world, we show that the love of God is not in us. "Do not love the world or the things in the world. If anyone loves the world, the love of the Father is not in him" (1 John 2:15).

Friendship with the world is death to the spiritual life and lethal poison to your fellowship with God's saints. You cannot love the world, turn around, and forgive others with God's love. Your love of the world will disqualify you from the quest to obey the Scriptures and aspire to peace in all your relationships. When it comes to the world and its pleasures, we should create the most outlandish hyperbole on a flashing neon sign, something like:

DANGER, DANGER, A THOUSAND DEATHS ARE IMMINENT!

There is so much knowledge and worldly wisdom. It is alluring and persuading, and the pride it generates is overwhelming. We must tether ourselves to Jesus; otherwise, our eyes will fill with the world's lust, the love of our hearts will be drawn away from what is holy, and we will become cold. Unity with others, ha! What a worthless pursuit.

Pride is the ruling spirit in our country. The American ideal of the self-made, independent (accountable to no one), and freedom-loving person is idolized in the archetype John Wayne character. He's iconic and masculine, taking on anyone, anytime, at the drop of a hat, with rugged individuality. These words, pride and individuality, are lived out daily across our country by Christians. They act out with selfish ambition, egotistical achievement, bombastic resume building, favoring image over authenticity, and excessive wealth accumulation, possessions, privacy, and secret lives.

Pride's most insidious form is spiritual pride. In *The Screwtape Letters*, Screwtape teaches Wormwood to tempt his male subject into adopting the strongest and most beautiful of vices—spiritual pride.[5] What could seem more outlandish than to call yourself Christian and yet have your character display the attributes and attitudes above? Forgiveness and seeking reconciliation. What for?

The words of this preceding paragraph are in acute contrast to the earnest follower of Jesus. "Jesus called the crowd together with His disciples, and said to them, 'If anyone wants to come after Me, he must deny himself, take up his cross, and follow Me'" (Mark 8:34, NASB). According to His example, the cross is the glory of Christ. And the cross becomes where our passions that feed our self and ego are crucified. Our swagger dissipates, and we boast only in the cross of our Lord Jesus (Gal. 6:14).

Thomas Merton prayed this holy prayer, which encapsulates many of these thoughts.

> But give me the strength that waits upon You in silence and peace. Give me humility in which alone is rest, and delivers me from pride which is the heaviest of burdens. And possess my whole heart and soul with the simplicity of love. Occupy my whole life with the one thought and the one desire of love, that I may love not for the sake of merit, not for the sake of perfection, not for the sake of virtue, not for the sake of sanctity, but for You alone.[6]

It is disheartening that this world's systems seep into the church and are enthusiastically embraced. The worldliness of the church today makes room for Christians to dismiss that "other" denomination with all its members (some who live next door to us). You must hope the Pentecostal person who speaks in tongues doesn't discover that you, the Baptist, live next door, or vice versa. Those labels immediately create separation as impassable as the Capertee Valley, the most expansive canyon on earth, located in New South Wales, Australia, with a width of nineteen miles![7]

The worldliness of the church allows Christian families to live in division, hurt, and bitterness. Bedevil the day a church leader would dare say to a member, "Wait a minute, you know that guy you sit near every Sunday, the one you won't speak to over some misunderstanding six years ago? You must get right with him before you take communion next week." The church rarely addresses grievances like this—these issues are personal and private. The church is expected to stay in its lane. It is this camaraderie with the world that T. Austin-Sparks saw and prophesied decades ago.

> The whole history of the church is one long story of this tendency to settle down on this earth and to become conformed to this world, to find acceptance and popularity here and to eliminate the element of conflict and pilgrimage. The more we come to our heavenly position, the more we find it impossible to allow man-made systems, which divide believers into groups, to operate and govern our lives.[8]

—T. AUSTIN-SPARKS

One of the notable marks of a disciple is that he is little a part of the world. The first disciples had united in the cross and the resurrection with Jesus. They belonged to another world, the kingdom of heaven, as should we. If we live as citizens of His kingdom, we will stand united.

Why is there such division in our relationships and families, and why is faith practiced so little today? We are too worldly—the world rules in the lives of too many Christians.

What about your community?

The word *authentic* is breathtaking. It carries such remarkable synonyms as genuine, accurate, bona fide, and honest. There is an ache in my heart for this kind of fellowship. I've experienced it on occasion. This fellowship with others is characterized by like-mindedness, having the same love, and being knit together in the Holy Spirit, intent on one purpose. I concede that all this sounds idealistic; however, all things are possible with God through the Holy Spirit. Authentic fellowship in the Spirit can become a divine reality, for it was God's intention in the first place and still stands today as His essential purpose.

This is where we find the most significant lack in our Christian experience for most of us. We lack genuine community with other believers. We may have an undisputable experience with Christ. However, the Christian life is not meant to exist with broken relationships and unforgiveness (strychnine to unity).

"Behold, how good and how pleasant it is for brothers to dwell together in unity!" (Ps. 133:1).

"Only let your conduct be worthy of the gospel of Christ, that whether or not I come and see you, I may hear of your activities, that you are standing fast in one spirit, with one mind, striving together for the faith of the gospel" (Phil. 1:27).

Be honest with yourself. Are there people in your fellowship who just bother you? Some are quirky, some obnoxious, others simply prickly. If you are like most people, you dodge these saints. God's grace does not allow us to experience fellowship in a make-believe world. It is His imperative that we live in the reality of others' dysfunctions and failures, people just like us. We live with an alien righteousness that allows us to come in unity with others through Jesus.

It is a complicated truth to expose. However, I have found the following to operate repeatedly in small groups. As a small group leader, I have encouraged others to join a fellowship. It is not unusual at all to see one of the members quietly, over a period, begin to withdraw and not attend. In watching the dynamics of people relating, it was evident that one in the group doesn't like someone's company. Many people think nothing of curtailing fellowship because they don't like someone, are poked by an obtuse personality, someone talking too much, or a myriad of other reasons. You can often see the impatience building in the person who quietly exits. He may cut the person off in conversations.

The reality is that too many Christians feel no responsibility to work at building relationships with others who are a little *different*. It is out of our comfort zone. I have witnessed this dissatisfied person attempt to marginalize the person they don't *like*. And if this is unsuccessful, they quietly head to the door. Their time is too valuable. They have their "feel-good" group and don't need anyone else. The reality of the whole situation is that they have sent a clear message, "I am superior to that Christian and don't need to tolerate them." Where is the discharge of our responsibility of simple brotherly love (Phil 2:3-4)?

A Special Word About Denominations

On a road trip of two-thousand-plus miles a few years ago, I had a lot of time to think. I reverted to listening to the radio, the only redemption being I chose a Christian channel. I was stunned and bewildered as I listened to one of the most outlandish conversations I have ever heard. A senior-level minister of a recognizable denomination was hosting a talk show and taking calls from members. The question-and-answer dialogue went something like this. The caller inquired about the advisability of visiting other evangelical churches. The immediate retort from the leader was terse and forceful. He touted that there could be only one purpose to visit another church: evangelization. I froze in disbelief at what I was hearing. However, he didn't stop there. He said it was a sin to consider leaving their denomination. For a moment, I didn't know if I was listening to a religious program, *The Twilight Zone*, or Nazi Germany propaganda.

Now it all made sense to me. When I was seventeen, a friend of mine's father sat me down, got out the Word of God, and showed me *the* truth. He explained why I would have to be rebaptized in their church to be saved. They were the only ones with a *proper* understanding of the Scriptures, and only their members would receive eternal life on the day of judgment.

E. Stanley Jones once wrote about the seven dangers to true fellowship.[9] Two of those were attempting to make fellowship an end to itself and making fellowship exclusive and self-superior. He argued that we end up making something relative, like fellowship, an absolute. In so doing, we have created an idol. He proposed that any group of people who believe they are unique, more righteous, or have a superior understanding of the Scriptures and God will invariably implode in their narrowness.

So stands the state of many of our denominations today. In their narrowness, they are losing relevance to modern Christian living. And in their allegiance to the denomination's beliefs, they have created a schism in the body of Christ that seems impossible. But it is not impenetrable. The Holy Spirit cannot be constrained, and we must pray for the gift of repentance to come to Christians.

We will only ever find unity through Christ. Different denominations and movements will never wholly agree on all points of doctrine. Paul says, "For as many as are led by the Spirit of God, these are the sons of God (Rom. 8:14). If the Spirit of God is leading us, we can discover unity with other Christians from various and sundry beliefs. Jesus never said we would know Christians by what they believe. Jesus clarified that we would know other followers of Him by their fruits (Matt. 7:15-20).

We must keep alert for the enemy's strategy to make the message of Jesus meaningless. And we now know his cunning move, the destruction of unity.

We think the world is not watching, but it is.

CHAPTER 7

THE OFFENSE— ENOUGH SAID

O My people, I have called thee to repentance and confession and forgiveness and cleansing; but ye have listened to My words as though they were but slight rustlings in the tree-tops—as though they were of little consequence and could be brushed aside at will.[1]

—FRANCES ROBERTS from *Come Away My Beloved*

Few strategies of Satan are more sinister and achieve more success for his end than offenses. Offenses are brutally potent; they hold Christians in chains for decades, some even well after the other party has died. Offenses can even pass on to subsequent generations, separating entire families. I've seen these firsthand, and I am sure you also have witnessed this vicious, destructive contrivance of the enemy.

What is this ominous stratagem that separates the closest of friends, alienates family members, splits churches, wrecks Christians' working relationships, and keeps the kingdom of heaven at bay? It is enticing to the immature Christian; it dupes those with the appearance of spiritual prowess; it ambushes the religious.

The Definition of Offense

Simply put, offense is a snare, stumbling block, and entrapment. People have reason to believe they have been mistreated; their conclusions are often mistaken for many reasons. Or someone has genuinely been harmed by another. In either case, unforgiveness sets in, and bitterness follows closely after that if it is not abated. After bitterness comes defilement in relationships. We can vividly remember the last bitter person we encountered; they left a foreboding impression.

When I started on this conquest to heal relationships and divisions in my life, it didn't take long to comprehend the nature of the divides. Offenses lie at the root of most, if not all, of my broken relationships. Some were small—a simple misunderstanding or massive. I terminated someone and was thus the evil accomplice of the devil. In some, I was the guilty person. But the level of the offense or its origination didn't seem to matter; the outcome was identical: separation and a broken relationship.

Embarking on the journey of reconciliation, I started listening closely to the stories of other Christians, most of whom live with broken relationships. I didn't have to travel far to hear these heartbreaking accounts of separation. Turning to my friends, I inquired and listened. What I heard was everything from startling to distressing: agony, trauma, depression, and every other imaginable negative emotion.

Listen with spiritual ears to what some of the Bible writers recorded about offense.

Jesus gave two direct warnings that offenses would come and keep coming.

But whoso shall offend one of these little ones which believe in me, it were better for him that a millstone were hanged about his neck, and that he were drowned in the depth of the sea.

Woe unto the world because of offences! for it must needs be that offences come; but woe to that man by whom the offence cometh!

—Matthew 18:6-7, KJV

Then said he unto the disciples, It is impossible but that offences will come: but woe unto him, through whom they come!

—Luke 17:1, KJV

Jesus could not have been more convincing in warning the disciples that offenses were serious and that being the one who offended any of God's children would bring terrible consequences. Let me be emphatic: This is Jesus speaking.

Solomon (the wisest man who ever lived, 1 Kings 3:12) also warned about offenses when he said, "A brother offended is harder to be won than a strong city: and their contentions are like the bars of a castle" (Prov. 18:19, KJV). In Solomon's day, a fortified city was considered one that had high walls next to impenetrable walls. Solomon's wisdom is on full display with this proverb.

Paul went as far as to instruct his young disciple Timothy about offenses. Paul warned him not to fall into the enemy's snare of contention, argument, and endless quarreling with those who opposed him. Here is the wise advice to Timothy from his elder sage.

And the Lord's servant must not be quarrelsome but must be kind to everyone, able to teach, not resentful. Opponents must be gently instructed, in the hope that God will grant them repentance leading them to a knowledge of the truth, and that they will come to their senses and escape from the trap of the devil, who has taken them captive to do his will.

—2 Timothy 2:24-26, NIV

Many Christians wear their emotions on their sleeves, have open wounds in the soul that make them easily hurt, and are prideful; some are just downright selfish, lovers of themselves just as Paul told Timothy (2 Tim. 3:2). It all appears like a setup for the enemy's most potent bait, offense. And with the level of division in our country, people seem primed, enticed, waiting to be offended. There is a spirit of offense that Satan has unleashed on our land. It hears things no one said and perceives an abusive remark when none was given. It is like piling on in football (if you are unfamiliar with the term, it means a runner has been tackled, but others just keep piling on). Matthew Henry was spot on in his commentary on Matthew 18:7-14 (see above), "Considering the cunning and malice of Satan, and the weakness and depravity of men's hearts, it is not possible but that there should be offenses."[2] Please read Matthew 8:7-14 in its entirety.

The enemy is at the zenith of his success as he cultivates offenses in the body of Christ. Christians grasp their offenses with a tight rein, refusing to release them. They hear sermon after sermon on forgiveness, love, and unity in the body yet somehow consider themselves exempt. Through offense, unforgiveness, pettiness, selfishness, envy, speculation, and hatred, Christians are blind to the overarching issue at hand—the witness we have before a dying world. Our lack of unity screams fraud, self-righteousness, and irrelevancy to the world.

The Multitude of Offenses

There exists such a variety of offenses it would be impossible to cover the gamut. Yet addressing some of these offenses will be invaluable to us. We can learn how not to be offended and assist others in recovering from the snare of offense. Most of us will face many of these examples; it is a grave truth and alarming expectation.

The Offense of Being Human, Those Little Foxes

You think I am jesting; I am not! By the time I became head of school at a Christian academy, I had worked in public education for fifteen years and, before that, in Christian higher education for ten years. I noticed something alarming about working in a Christian organization instead of a public/secular enterprise. What was it? The expectation of perfection, finding heaven on earth, and experiencing eternal bliss at work. Employees couldn't have been more unrealistic in what they thought they would find working in a Christian organization. Many employees were being set up for a colossal disappointment and offense. Many had worked in the public sector or public school system and assumed they would walk into the third heaven at a Christian school. Their expectations were dashed the first time they had a bad day or someone upset them or didn't speak to them like an angel.

I gravitated to making a portion of the new-employee orientation around the issue of expectations of perfection from the Christian school. I assigned each new employee to read *A Tale of Three Kings* by Gene Edwards. It is the most pointed book I have come across that addresses how a Christian is to respond to flawed leadership. I told each of the new employees, one-on-one, to be prepared; at some point, I will disappoint you. If not me, then someone else. It was inevitable; we are human. We are imperfect; there is only One who is perfect.

So many believers face this reality and often succumb to the expectation that our Christian brothers and sisters will act like saints on all occasions. They will not, you will not; we are all works in progress. We are pressing on to the mark of the high calling in Christ Jesus. We are empowered by the Holy Spirit and doing our best to follow His suggestions as we walk through each day.

The question is, do you allow people just to be human? To be honest, we have dozens of opportunities every day to be offended by the actions of others. People can be selfish, indifferent, insensitive, and inattentive, and they can expose many other negative qualities that create the perfect storm for offense. Maybe you are that person now and then.

Those little devilish offenses take so little to offend us: a person's quirks, a smirk, or a misunderstanding. Most offenses begin in such small, subtle ways. In the Song of Solomon, the speaker tells his bride-to-be, "Catch the foxes for us, the little foxes that spoil the vineyards, for our vineyards are in blossom" (Song 2:15). In the middle of this beautiful, romantic allegory, why does the thought of little foxes come up? Why does he entreat his beloved to catch them? The foxes are symbolic. They are the ones who can spoil the vine while it is blossoming. They could dismantle the budding relationship between the couple.

The enemy's devices to create division are as subtle as they are persistent. Offenses spring up like weeds in a garden. These little foxes separate the closest, most devoted friends and casual acquaintances. Just as we must guard our hearts, we must be on guard to not allow these little foxes of offense to demolish our relationships.

Two excellent secretaries worked side by side for years in a middle school. They were both employed there before I became principal. These women attended church and were known for their kindness and hard work. Then it happened: an offense came between them. As I visited with them together and separately, they needed help identifying the problem. The best I could determine was that they arrived at the place where familiarity allowed them to see each other's quirks, and these peculiarities of personality resulted in offense. It was disheartening; nothing I said or tried could ease the tension. Almost every teacher in the school became pointedly aware of the disunity in the office. The teachers had to live with this conflict as they had to interact with the office almost daily. Every day students observed and felt the tension, and all the while the enemy gloated as the secretaries' Christian witness disappeared. I went so far as to move out of my office and create a standing desk from which I worked to officiate their offense. It failed. I finally turned hardline and threatened to dismiss them if it persisted. I was never told what they did, but they quickly resolved the offense between them.

One of the most profound ways to elude offense from these "little foxes" is to avoid speculating. I can hear the shutters as people are reading this. It seems natural to speculate. Dr. Jeff Beyer says, "When we speculate we judge others. We need to make love our goal and our heart offense proof."[3] Wow! One of the propensities I've noticed about speculating is that people rarely speculate a positive thought; instead, they assume the worst outcome.

Massive Offense

Massive offenses are the polar opposite of the "little foxes." Massive offenses are the most difficult to overcome. Many of us, if not all, have had the horrific experience of a massive offense. It brings your life to a halt and can take you captive. These hideous invitations to bondage attack us in unimaginable ways.

- You discover by accident your spouse is in a sexual relationship.

- A fellow employee accuses you wrongly to your employer. They are secretly jealous of you because you stand in their career path.

- The confidences you shared with a trusted spiritual advisor are shared with others.

- You are the victim of physical or sexual abuse.

- The executor of your parents will (your sibling) is taking every opportunity to take advantage of their responsibilities for personal gain.

- Your spouse has a gambling addiction, and you discover your life's savings are gone, and you are tens of thousands of dollars in credit card debt.

- You are sued unjustly by a business partner.

- Your child is being sexually harassed.

Unimaginable offenses

- A parent loses their only daughter to a drunk driver.

- A man who lost decades of his life behind bars was falsely imprisoned and is finally freed.

- A shooter attacks the Amish community's one-room schoolhouse, and five girls lose their lives.

These examples are painful to write, and the different actions that led to these massive offenses seem innumerable. Sadly, these behaviors are almost normative in our homes, churches, and society. The outcomes of these disastrous events for most Christians are dramatic offense and unforgiveness. If unforgiveness persists, the person's capacity for fellowship becomes limited. The offended ostensibly justify their unforgiveness because of the horrific degree of hurtfulness from these massive assaults.

Please don't interpret my observations as a lack of understanding and compassion for those who have suffered massive offenses. I experienced sexual abuse as a young teen, was sued unjustly, and lost hundreds of thousands of dollars because of a relative's gambling addiction. But I too have been the offender through sinful actions not surrendered to the Lord. I am humiliated and humbled by my sins but forgiven and cleansed by the blood of Jesus. And I have done my best (Rom. 12:18) to seek forgiveness and live at peace with others.

Massive offenses become one of the most significant opportunities to trust and yield to God's will. I am not under any illusion that one can simply walk away from a massive offense and quickly forgive, having taken years on one occasion to forgive a betrayal. Yet, by seeking God daily for forgiveness, massive offenses can be forgiven.

By God's grace, Corrie ten Boom forgave one of the brutal Nazi German prison guards. She recognized him from the Ravensbrück concentration camp when he walked up to her years later after a meeting where she was speaking and sought her forgiveness.[4] How did Corrie forgive this sinful man from the place where she and her sister were abused and her sister died? By the blood and power of Jesus.

Maria Goretti was born a poor peasant child in Italy in 1890. She was assaulted and then stabbed fourteen times. She survived for twenty hours in the hospital, undergoing surgery without anesthesia, and before dying, said of her assailant, "Yes, for the love of Jesus I forgive him...and I want him to be with me in Paradise." The vicious man was sentenced to thirty years in prison and eleven years later had visions of Maria that caused him to turn to Christ. After serving twenty-eight years in prison, his first act was to seek Maria's mother to forgive him, and then he dedicated the rest of his life to a Capuchin monastery. Maria was canonized in a ceremony attended by a quarter million people, including her mother, the first mother ever to see her child canonized.[5]

That Amish community. The gunman, a milk truck driver, shot ten young girls, killing five, then himself. The community and individual families have grieved for years, likely even today. But their immediate response has inspired thousands. They forgave the shooter, and the community donated money to the killer's widow and three young children.[6]

These are extreme examples of forgiveness; they seemingly allowed justifiable grounds for unforgiveness and offense. But these examples of forgiveness help us visualize that there is no offense so great that God's grace does not reach further. Every act of forgiveness sets someone free from a prison or a potential prison. It could be the offender, the offended, or both; forgiveness always releases someone into freedom.

Forgiveness from massive offenses isn't saying the offense was OK; it is saying I release you to God. He is the one who judges you, not me. The Holy Spirit gives us the strength to forgive even massive offenses. He says to us, ask. Ask again and again. He helps us in our weaknesses (Rom. 8:26-28). But we must ask.

Offenses in the Church

Unmet expectations and expectations of perfection are rampant in the church. The pastor, the worship leader, and the youth worker are scrutinized with microscopic attention. They cannot win; they are, after all, human, just like us. We are doomed to be offended when we hold on to this expectation of perfection in our leadership as a condition of fellowship. Jesus did not choose twelve perfect men; there weren't any around then, and there aren't any now.

The church seems to create an atmosphere similar to what I wrote about in the Christian organizations where I worked. However, the church may be an even riper setting for offense. Most church people are acquaintances and don't understand or appreciate the nuances (idiosyncrasies) of others' personalities.

What are we to do about these and the many other offenses that happen in the church? If we are the offended party, we must first pray. But we can't stop there. We must ask the Lord what He wants to do for us through this situation. The Lord is gracious to work in everything we encounter (the good and the bad) if we turn to Him. He wants us to mature and grow as disciples. I have discovered that in most of my experiences with offense, misunderstandings, and hurt feelings, if I enter the relationship pointing the finger, three are pointing back at me. Try it; point your finger and observe the three pointing back at you. However, if after much prayer we believe the Spirit of God wants us to address what has taken place that we don't like, two things need to happen: 1) We must take a deep check into our spirit and ask God to help us go to the offender with the humility of Jesus, and 2) we must learn how to inquire, not accuse, and make a godly appeal.

The last line of verse 1 John 1:7, "and the blood of Jesus his Son cleanses us from all sin," is our hope for fellowship. It is a realization we must all come to. As my pastor Jon says, "My life is too big for me. There is no hope for me in me. I must have Jesus." Leviticus instructs us that "the blood is the life" (Lev. 17). This life is lived out in the sacrifice of Jesus and His blood being shed. Only through Jesus' sacrifice and the work of the Holy Spirit can we hope to realize unity.

The Abuse of Spiritual Power and Corrupt Christian Leadership

Every one of us has power in some sphere almost daily, yet we may not even be aware of it. Get behind the wheel of a car and you will witness first-hand the abuse of power. Autos are dangerously forceful, and with some people, the only form of power they can wield in life. And they do—they wield it, swerving in and out of traffic, speeding, and tailgating unmercifully. Whether in this abuse of the force of a car or the misuse of power in relationships, we have all felt its sting. And perhaps we have been the stinger. However, being the recipient of abuse from someone in spiritual authority is pain at a deeper level in our hearts.

If you have spent much time in church, you likely have felt the prick of abuse by a leader or the disappointment in corrupt leadership. Leadership is the term that is in vogue in the Christian world today, and you don't have to look far to see the new and inventive, cutting-edge, and impactful Christian leadership conferences or training schools. However, I have noticed a grave deficiency in most leadership training. There doesn't seem to be a crucial focus on teaching how to steward power, let alone accountability.

Whether in the little country church or the most extensive Christian discipleship training program, position and title bring power in practically every Christian setting. On the heels of this power is the ability to influence how others act. Power can be a crucial component of a leader's capacity to do good; however, it can be devastatingly wielded for selfishness and harm to others. "Nothing is more useful than power, nothing more frightful."[7]

Oh, have we witnessed the abuses of power in the church today! Ministers exercise power to promote their agenda, almost always tied to monetary gain and wealth. A church official is sexually abusing others. The lurid accounts of sexual exploitation leave a wake of devastation to the offended and disillusionment to the observers.

Have you felt the helplessness that comes from being abused by the power of a Christian leader? Have you suffered disappointment when your favorite pastor or Bible teacher is exposed as a narcissistic fraud? Too many of us can answer an unequivocal yes. Christine Westoff could not be more accurate, "The greater the power, the greater the temptation. The greater the power, the less accountability."[8]

On the heels of abuse arises the opportunity for offense. The pump is primed and ready to gush forth offense and separation.

A straightforward way to safeguard yourself from being hurt by a Christian leader and the opportunity for offense that follows so quickly is to guard your heart. Your heart is where every issue in life flows from (Prov. 4:23). But let me make this distinction clear: I am not saying be guarded, unwilling or reluctant to embrace relationships. There is a vast difference between being guarded and using the discernment and wisdom of the Spirit to guard what enters your heart and mind.

We must recognize the place of prayer and the Word of God when overcoming offense. These two Christian disciplines equip us to stand firm and unoffended. We pray to connect with our Lord and Savior and, secondly, to get answers to prayer. And the Word of God is abounding with promises to assist us.

"There is such a great peace and well-being that comes to the lovers of your Word, and they will never be offended" (Ps. 119:165, TPT).

"The unfolding of your words gives light; it gives understanding to the simple. I open my mouth and pant, longing for your commands. Turn to me and have mercy on me, as you always do to those who love your name. Direct my footsteps according to your word; let no sin rule over me (Ps. 119:130-133, NIV).

A Word on Enemies

When you experience an event and think it will result in the worst offense, another offense crops up that trumps it. When you climb the ladder of offenses, few surpass the seemingly irreversible offense that can come from an enemy. And when an enemy is victorious and damages your family, livelihood, reputation, or any other personal item, you face what seems a natural response: *to seek revenge.*

What is an enemy? *Merriam-Webster* defines it as "one seeking to injure, overthrow, or confound an opponent. Something harmful or deadly."[9] The essence of an enemy is that they intentionally, often calculatedly, attempt to injure or destroy you.

Have you ever had an enemy? If you have, you realize there seems to be no end to people's wickedness. I'm surprised that many people I ask that question of say no, *not that they know of.* But here is the rub: Most enemies work in the unseen and backrooms. They belittle you to others and spread rumors, or they can undermine you in a thousand other ways.

What about these examples? Would you consider any of these to be enemies?

- You discover someone has lied to the pastor of your church about your past.

- A coworker takes credit for your work and then plants a seed of distrust in the boss.

- A woman repeatedly makes passes at your husband.

- A neighbor on your block that you do not know threatens your children.

What do you do with an enemy? The opportunity for offense is off the charts. How can you withstand this kind of offense and not respond negatively? You may think, "No man has ever been treated so unjustly." Let's return to the Lord's Prayer and how Jesus taught us, as His disciples, to pray: "and forgive us our sins, as we have forgiven those who sin against us." (Matt. 6:12, NLT). And when the Lord's Prayer concludes, Jesus says: "If you have forgiven those who sin against you, your heavenly Father will forgive you. But if you refuse to forgive others, your Father will not forgive your sins" (Matt. 6:14-15, NLT).

But Jesus doesn't stop here. He continually calls us to enlighten deeper places in our hearts we are not aware of, as St. Augustine of Hippo prayed,

O Holy Spirit, love of God,
pour out your grace,
and descend plentifully into my heart.
Enlighten the dark corners of this neglected dwelling,
and scatter there your cheerful beams.[10]

Jesus elevates the thought of forgiving our enemies to a standard that can only be achieved through intimacy with Him and the Holy Spirit. Jesus gives us His love, and the Holy Spirit strengthens us.

Jesus proclaims with total clarity and unapologetically that we must love our enemies. "You have heard it said, 'Love your neighbor and hate your enemy.' But I tell you, love your enemies and pray for those who persecute you, that you may be children of your Father in heaven" (Matt. 5:43,44, 45a, NIV).

Let me be as clear as I am able. **Forgiving the offenses of others, from minor to massive, is in no way excusing the behavior.** But it does mean dealing a death blow to everything in us that screams for that person to be hurt as they have hurt us. God has the remedy we need to conquer all offenses, the love of Christ shed abroad in our hearts through the Holy Spirit. "Hatred stirs up strife, but love covers all offenses (Prov. 10:12, NASB).

We have to be ever so careful when it comes to offense. Too often we make decisions based on a natural response to relieve our pressure or pain. However, the steps we take may not be the actions God desires. And this particularly applies in a church setting. Many people are easily offended and wander from church to church; they become spiritual vagabonds.

Finally, herein lies one of the supreme proofs of our earnestness in following Jesus: Will we forgive others who offend us as freely as God has forgiven us?

Forgiveness is a willful act, an act of surrender. Our wills may not be strong, but they can surrender.

CHAPTER 8

DON'T SHUT THE DOOR WITH YOUR WORDS

Morally and spiritually, we live, as it were, in sections, and the door from one section to another is by means of words, and until we say the right word the door will not open.[1]

—OSWALD CHAMBERS

Jesus told the parable of the soils from a boat to a large crowd standing on a shore (Matt. 13). The disciples didn't understand why Jesus spoke in parables and didn't understand this parable. Away from the crowd, Jesus proceeded to tell His disciples the meaning of the parable of the soils. When it came to the good soil that would yield fruit, He said, "But the seed falling on good soil refers to someone who hears the word and understands it. This is the one who produces a crop, yielding a hundred, sixty or thirty times what was sown" (Matt. 13:23b, NIV). Notice that Jesus said, "and understands it."

I believe Jesus wants you to gain a new understanding of the weight of your words; this is crucial to every relationship you have. In the quote above by Oswald Chambers, he speaks prophetically to us today: "You need to speak the right words to open the doors to restoration in your relationship(s)."

We live in a world of toxic, verbal pollution. Our culture seemingly slams the door Chambers speaks of in the face of all the components necessary for life-giving communication. Day after day we encounter people with no moral compass or safe boundaries with the *words* that cross their lips. And to make it insufferable, that includes the way too many Christians talk. No wonder relationship offenses are rampant and division exists in our land. Offensive words are shouted in your ear at every turn.

The enemy of our soul is in the middle of the massacre of this exquisite tool, language. Words like propriety, modesty, politeness, and respectfulness seem to be disemboweled from our vocabulary. Satan is insidiously attacking our hearts and minds, attempting to morph our words that bring peace, comfort, and life into his words that steal harmony and instigate discord between people. The freedom that too many Christians use to speak their minds is utterly irresponsible and not the freedom Christ died for on the cross. God had a purpose when He created man for fellowship and unity. And this is the reason we have His very language to communicate His love.

However, I firmly believe there is a different path for Jesus' followers, and the doorway to that path is wide open. So brace yourself to hear things you may not have heard before. I trust these words I write will energize and encourage you on this passageway to life, words that open doors to unity.

We can easily understand how creative, breathtaking, and commanding God's words are. Bask in the first four words God spoke in the Scriptures, "And then God announced, 'Let there be light, and light burst forth!'"

(Gen 1:3, TPT). The consequence of God's ineffable words was to generate electromagnetic waves, the laws of physics, radiation, and all other essential contributors to the materialization of light. What if God didn't just create us in His image but also gave us His very means of communication? Think about the potential power in our words. Mind-boggling!

Most of us understand the power of positive words and their impact. If you are like me, you have an inner craving for affirmation and to know people care about you—these thoughts are best expressed through words. I say that positive words are like verbal nutrients to our soul. Whole Christian movements and ministries are founded on the power of positive words and confessions. But I believe that we have not fully understood the dramatic power of negative words in marriage, relationships, and with Christian friends. Negative words in these settings catalyze hurt feelings and misunderstandings that lead to separation.

Drunk with Words

A few years back, I noticed a pattern in the Book of Proverbs. Proverbs is called "wisdom literature."[2] Specifically, Proverbs is often identified as Solomon's wisdom. I studied Proverbs, chapter by chapter and line by line. In so doing, I discovered that twenty-three out of the thirty-one Proverbs chapters are more about words than wisdom. Proverbs could be renamed *The Power of Words* (don't hold your breath on that happening). However, the relevant fact for our study is that of those twenty-three chapters on words, many more are about the power of negative words than positive words.

Negative words plant seeds of distrust in relationships. It is sobering and chilling the way Christians manipulate and mutilate language in ungodly ways. I penned a book, *The Forty-Day Word Fast*, about the most destructive words in our language: judgments, criticism, sarcasm, complaining, and gossip. I am stunned at the response from the tens of thousands of

Christians who have read my book. I read account after account of the effects of uncontrolled language that mimics the world's rhetoric, leading to estrangement in families, relationships, and church division.

Scripture contains sobering admonitions regarding the words that cross our lips and cause rifts and offense. From warnings about uncontrolled speech to the chilling impact of these negative words (judgments, criticism, sarcasm, complaining, and gossip), God's Word could not be more penetrating. Read God's words in James and ask yourself this painful question: Is my religion worthless?

> If anyone thinks himself to be religious, yet does not bridle his tongue but deceives his *own* heart, this person's religion is worthless.
>
> —James 1:26, NASB

As I read this verse and other scriptures such as James 3:1-12, James 4:11, or Proverbs 6:16-19, I regularly say to others, "Could God mean what He is saying?" Could my loose tongue negate all my religious activity and fervor? It doesn't take me long to rebut, come to my senses, and realize the answer is obvious: YES. God's invitation to everyone is to submit our lives to Him, particularly the words that cross our lips. Honoring, obeying, and submitting to God's Word through the power of the Holy Spirit will produce life and harmony in relationships. And we can't simply pass over chilling thoughts like Proverbs 6:16-19; it is an unreserved warning to those who sow discord among brothers.

> There are six things which the LORD hates, seven that are an abomination to Him: Haughty eyes, a lying tongue, and hands that shed innocent blood, a heart that devises wicked plans, feet that run rapidly to evil, a false witness who declares lies, and one who spreads strife among brothers.
>
> —Proverbs 6:16-19, NASB

Back to these masters of disaster in our relationships: judgments, criticism, sarcasm, complaining, and gossip. Let me articulate more thoroughly what I understand about the disunity these words create. Most of us need constant reminders that these negative words are not in God's vocabulary. They are Satan's perverted distortion of God's original intention. C. S. Lewis stated emphatically the profound result of these injurious words. "When we Christians behave badly or fail to behave well, we are making Christianity unbelievable to the outside world."[3]

Judgments, Criticism, Sarcasm, Complaining, and Gossip

Judgments

We judge people in two ways. First, we think we know what is in their heart and mind, their motivation, their thoughts, and why they do what they do. How remarkably arrogant and what dramatic deception! Who do we think we are, God?

> The heart is more deceitful than all else and is desperately sick; who can understand it? I, the LORD, search the heart, I test the mind, to give to each person according to his ways, according to the results of his deeds.
>
> —Jeremiah 17:9-10, NASB

How can we be in accord with others when constantly judging them?

However, the second way we judge is even more destructive to relationships: evaluating a person's value, quality, or worth. There is little chance we could be in harmony with others to whom we judge and ascribe value. Be honest with yourself. When was the last time you judged someone (today)?

My wife and I have recently been pressing in on this issue of not judging others. And we are discovering a marvelous, more profound level of freedom in our Christian life. Many Christians do not recognize the prison that judgments create in their lives. If you judge, you are a captive, incapable of a healthy marriage, enriching friendships, and unity with other believers. But it gets worse, much worse. The Scriptures make us this unenviable promise: You will emphatically be judged in the measure you judge others (Matt. 7:1-2).

How do I stop this reckless judging of others?

My answer starts here: "So from now on we regard no one from a worldly point of view. Though we once regarded Christ in this way, we do so no longer. Therefore, if anyone is in Christ, the new creation has come: The old has gone, the new is here!" (2 Cor. 5:16-17, NIV)

When I started dealing with my judgmental attitude, I immediately recognized how deceived I was. I made decisions by judging others in my mind and often without voicing what I was thinking. Here are a few examples of judgmental thoughts. See if any of these thoughts hit home with you.

- Is that person limping just to draw attention to themselves? (It's embarrassing, but I remember the specific place and time when that thought crossed my mind.)
- My grandpa is stingy.
- My boss is a total narcissist.
- Our new worship leader sure is standoffish.
- That driver who cut in front of me is an idiot!

It is such an easy (natural?) trap to fall into, drawing conclusions on others fashioned around a few actions. When we do this, we are relating to people from a worldly point of view—according to the flesh (see the scripture above). However, with the help of the Holy Spirit, you can change the habit of judging and become an observer who uses the discernment of the Holy Spirit. This is how the normal Christian life plays out for most of us. Rarely does a day pass when you don't need to decide important matters.

- Do I let my twelve-year-old have a sleepover with a Christian friend from church?

- Can I trust someone in my small group at church and be vulnerable about a personal need?

- Does my boss really want me to be honest about areas of improvement I see the company needs?

How do I make these decisions without unfairly judging someone and instead using the discernment of the Spirit? I realize this may be a new thought to you: Become an observer in life and relationships. Let's start with self-awareness. God wants us to learn to walk in the Spirit throughout our day. This is an essential step in learning to be an observer and curtail judging. We need the sensitivity and discernment of the Spirit. This can be worked into our lives as we seek the Spirit to guide our thoughts, the words that come out of our mouths, and our actions.

Back to that observer. When you observe, look for the fruits in someone's life to make the decisions you need to make every day. "But the fruit of the Spirit is love, joy, peace, forbearance, kindness, goodness, faithfulness, gentleness, and self-control. Against such things there is no law" (Gal. 5:22-23, NIV).

Whether or not I allow my daughter to sleep over at a friend's house depends on the love and peace observed in that family's home.

Whether or not I trust someone in my small group with a personal need will depend on how I observe their faithfulness with the information shared.

Observing my boss's self-control and kindness in response to a coworker's mistake may help me determine whether he wants to hear my suggestions for improving the company.

When making a critical decision, we look for the fruits of the Spirit. We are not looking for how often someone goes to church, whether someone is in a small group, or whether the boss says to a large group he wants suggestions on improving the company.

When walking in the Spirit and observing the fruit in other people's lives, you stop trying to peer into a person's heart. You are no longer deceived into thinking you can know a person's motivation. The result is simple: You observe.

Here's an example of the discernment of the Holy Spirit in action versus judging. Just this past Sunday, Annamae took me to our favorite Mexican restaurant. The waitress delivered the customary chips and salsa and took our drink order. Later, she took our food orders and delivered them when it came up. As lunch was winding down, Annamae told me our waitress was hurting. I believe something is wrong with her. I was clueless as to what she was saying. I just assumed (judged) that the woman was not a good waitress. I had to catch her to get extra chips. She didn't ask if I needed a second drink.

Annamae took the waitress's hand when she returned to the table to deliver our check and asked, "Are you hurting?" She answered yes. I could see it in her eyes by then. She was obviously in pain. Annamae proceeded to pray for her and leave an extra generous tip. That's what walking in the Spirit looks like. Do you want some of that? Drench yourself in the Word, pray, and have quiet times with the Lord, spending most of the time still and listening.

You will make great discoveries and an astonishing leap upward into being taught by the Spirit. The Spirit will teach you to walk after the Spirit and not make decisions after the flesh.

Criticism

When we criticize others, we are expressing disapproval or fault finding. We are not building someone up; we are tearing them down. A person with a critical spirit is insatiable and knows no boundaries. They are critical of their spouse, children, friends (if they have any), the minister at church, and on and on *ad nauseum*. They are offending people at every turn.

Who wants to be around a critical person? No one! Critical people are gloomy and miserable. They throw a dark cloud over every relationship they have. Almost every one of us knows or has known a critical person (maybe that was you before you met Christ). We can all relate to the immense challenge of spending time around a critical person. The more painful challenge comes when that critical person is in your close family or someone you work with.

Criticism has become a standard, habitual element of our culture. As Christians, many of us have become desensitized to the critical rants we hear about other people, in particular, anyone in leadership or an elected position. If we fall in line with the world and develop a critical spirit, we will live separated from so many people, including Christians. Many Christ followers think they can separate their critical tirades about non-Christians, politicians, or Christians outside their community setting from their spiritual life and witness. I don't believe this is possible. Criticism, if embraced, will bleed into every domain of a person's existence. And most Christians fail to understand this subtle, egregious destroyer of relationships on every level: family, friends, fellowship, and social relationships. That destructive force? Silent criticism.

Once forged with a spouse, community of believers, or close family members, fellowship can be a dramatic strength when the storms of life come from without. Christians can be seemingly supernatural in surrounding and supporting members of their tribe. But Christian fellowship and unity are tender and susceptible to pressures from within. The little bores that eat at the heart of a tree or ravage its fruit are analogous to the damage done by secret criticism to the unity of believers.

It isn't often that I would be so bold as to say I have a word from the Lord on an issue. But I do. Read this thoughtfully because we are spiritual beings, and the operation of the Spirit is in the unseen. Secret criticism is strychnine to Christian fellowship. Even if we have no idea someone is harboring secret criticism in their heart against us, our spirits will be separated. Secret criticism will thwart authenticity in relationships. And it will obstruct the fellowship in the Spirit at every juncture.

Our secret criticism of others often comes out on full display—and is no longer hidden—through social media. In subtle or not-so-subtle postings, Christians are critical and rant about others. It is as if being behind a screen provides anonymity or detachment of personal responsibility for the words posted.

When the Holy Spirit reveals that you are harboring secret criticism toward someone, there is only one apt response. Confess the criticism for what it is: sin. Seek forgiveness from the Lord.

Sarcasm

My wife and I were in a prayer time with couples recently. I noticed that the husband of one of the couples (I'll call him Fred) engaged people with a sarcastic bent. This bent was obvious when Fred attempted humor, which he did often. His humor was always at the expense of someone else present. Annamae shared her experience, which I had heard her share before. It was a tremendous encouragement about walking in the Spirit. Fred quickly took her sharing and added a humorous, sarcastic comment. He hastily realized how out of place his comment was and tried to backtrack. However, the sarcasm immediately deflated the sweet spirit in the atmosphere of our prayer time.

Our culture praises sarcasm. And because it is so widespread, we have become jaded by its mean-spiritedness, rudeness, and offense. So many Christians emulate the world's sense of humor; its invitation is subtle and seductive. However, the unceasing, brutal, sarcastic bantering about those in authority is wearying. The more sarcastic you are, the cleverer people take you to be. I'm sure you have noticed how sarcastic humor dominates many sectors of our society. Try on some of these quips.

- You're not pretty enough to be this stupid.

- You're the human equivalent of a participation award.

- He is not the sharpest tool in the workshop.

- The pastor had a great sermon today. Where did he get it?

When people make these kinds of comments to someone or about someone behind their back, they are perpetuating Satan's plan to disempower fellowship and instigate chasms between Christians. Those who use this earthy sarcasm have become the conduit of the enemy. I implore you today to be bold, discerning, humble, and repentant if sarcasm is part of your verbal repertoire.

Complaining

People are going to complain. Right. They will complain about waiting in line, their spouse, the guy in front of them in traffic, the slow computers, the mailman, the pastor, the worship leader, the boss, and so on. Egad, do people complain. But what most Christians don't comprehend about complaining is that it quenches the Spirit. The Spirit will not be present when the atmosphere is rife with complaining.

How does complaining diffuse fellowship and create a division among believers? Here is the answer and one of the most important lessons I have ever learned: The Holy Spirit is easily quenched. I need to discover what I do that quenches the Spirit in my personal life and relationships and not do those things.

Complaining sends a clear message to God: "I don't trust You. I don't believe You have things under control." It casts doubt and sends all the wrong communication to Him. Complaining will have the same effects on you that it had on the Israelites as they grumbled their way through their forty-year wilderness jaunt in the desert. They murmured, wailed, disapproved, and depreciated God. Worst of all, they grew ungrateful. Their constant complaining stalled and finally obliterated their pathway to the Promised Land. They did not fulfill God's purpose for their families. This is the fruit of complaining: not being able to steward relationships and experience the intimacy with God and others that He planned for you before you were in your mother's womb. Complaining will always quench the Spirit.

We are on the wrong train if we think we can complain, whine, and grumble yet be devoted disciples of Jesus and live in harmony with others. Complaining strikes at the heart of God. It questions God's goodness and recants God's nature and glory. When Moses asked to see God's glory, God responded, "I will make my goodness pass before you" (Exod. 33:19).

If you find yourself on the tram of a complaining lifestyle, there is a way off. Find something to be grateful for. Start looking for good in the people around you. You will find plenty to appreciate and praise. Approach your relationships with this attitude: Lord, open my eyes to the best in people.

The Holy Spirit of God invites you to experience a lifestyle without complaining. Oh, the sweetness you will rediscover in your fellowship with other Christians. If you are married, your spouse will be the first to notice the difference.

Gossip

In chapter 11, "The Twin Demons of Destruction," I will address gossip for the spiritual butcher it is. It commands more comprehensive attention because it is one of the enemy's choicest weapons. Here is a foretaste of the gravitas of this salacious marauder.

In a homily during the first year of his pontificate, Pope Francis said that a Christian who gossips is a murderer. "A Christian murderer...it's not me saying this, it's the Lord. And there is no place for nuances. If you speak ill of your brother, you kill your brother. And every time we do this, we are imitating that gesture of Cain, the first murderer in history."[4]

Will Somebody Listen to Me?

As much as we talk about communication (words) in educational circles, I am still waiting to see anyone at any level teach the components of listening. I pray you learn to listen when there is a conflict or offense. No, I mean really listen. Cut the words; stop talking and give the other person your full attention.

I remember when a parent left my office after unloading on me about a teacher. This parent complained about many things, so I took her anger with a bit of incredulity. But something unique happened as soon as she left. The Spirit of the Lord spoke to me, "Did you hear her? No, did you really hear her?" The short of it was I had not. But another chance came soon. There she was, waiting on me at my assistant's desk a few days later, and she was as mad as a wet hornet (ouch). However, this time I sat down with her, looked her straight in the eyes, gave her my complete attention (I forewarned my assistant not to interrupt me and to hold all calls), and put my cell phone on mute.

Something near miraculous occurred. As I sat there, I could feel the hurt and emotional wounds of this child of God. It was the first time I understood that when someone says they are angry, they are probably angry. And I began to pray that something would take place in the spirit realm, that in her spirit she would perceive my spirit's sincere desire to assist her, as best I could. This woman's relationship began to change with the school, but the most significant change that day transpired in me. I embarked on a journey to become a better listener. It has been quite a ride along the way, not what I thought it would be.

There is a starting point in healing relationships. It is the place of listening. Yes, we need to be able to speak the correct words, words that seek forgiveness and offer forgiveness. But these words will best come from right listening to God and then taking the time to really listen to others.

Heartfelt listening is a majestic ministry we can offer to others. It will break the husk of indifference, reticence, and standoffishness we often encounter in broken relationships. I implore you to make it a personal goal to improve your listening skills. It is a spiritual endeavor that will reap the marvelous fruit of deepening your current relationships and helping you reconnect with broken ones. Here are a few essential thoughts on listening.

- To listen, you must close your mouth and pray to God to open your ears.

- Be quiet, and you will cease to judge and condemn others.

- Turn off every instinct to talk about yourself.

- Make it your goal to be skilled in asking deep-hearted questions.

Brothers and sisters in Christ, I have discovered that few things confront impatience and selfishness as much as learning to listen. It will be the same for you.

In Summary

In the letter to the Ephesian church, the apostle Paul repeatedly gives the Christians examples of how they should live. He particularly instructs them to do away with filthy talk, anger, quarreling, malice, insults, and crude joking. Paul encourages them to let their words instead encourage one another with kindness and grace, and most importantly to graciously forgive each other.

Let no unwholesome word proceed out of your mouth, but only that which is good for building up, that it may give grace to the listeners. And do not grieve the Holy Spirit of God, in whom you are sealed for the day of redemption. Let all bitterness, wrath, anger, outbursts, and blasphemies, with all malice, be taken away from you. And be kind one to another, tenderhearted, forgiving one another, just as God in Christ also forgave you.

—Ephesians 4:29-32

When we participate in sinful actions with our tongue, we are doing Satan's bidding and accusing the saints before God. Let us humble ourselves and repent. Negative words and thoughts are an outward sign of what resides in our hearts.

A good man brings good things out of the good stored up in his heart, and an evil man brings evil things out of the evil stored up in his heart. For the mouth speaks what the heart is full of.

—Luke 6:45, NIV

True intimacy and unity can come anytime Christians walk free of judging, criticizing, using sarcasm, complaining, and gossiping about each other and instead pray for and listen to each other. You can experience the joyful, Spirit-filled life of Christ in your relationships.

CHAPTER 9

BREAKING THE SWORD

O Lord, deliver me from this lust of always vindicating myself.[1]

—ST. AUGUSTINE OF HIPPO

The Enemy's Weapons

Ephesians 6:10-20 are the most familiar scriptures about the armor God has given us to protect against the enemy's schemes. Though most people say there is just one offensive weapon in this passage, I believe there are two: the Sword of the Spirit, which is the Word of God (Rom. 6:17), and Spirit-empowered prayer (Rom. 6:18). However, guess who else has potent spiritual weapons? Satan.

That's right, the devil, the enemy of your soul. Those are names you don't hear often at church. Most ministers have very little to say about Satan and spiritual warfare today. If you desire to maintain credibility with most of your Christian friends, it's not something to bring up in conversations. Far too many Christians scoff at the thought of the devil, Satan, the enemy—however you choose to identify that fallen angel.

How do you think most Christians would react if you told them, "I have an ailment that has not responded to doctor's treatment. I believe it is a thorn in the flesh sent from Satan meant to beat me down and cause suffering" (2 Cor. 12:7)? Or what if you said to a Christian brother with whom you have been trying to meet to resolve a misunderstanding, "The devil keeps putting up roadblocks that keep me from meeting with you" (1 Thess. 2:18)? Hmm. Do you think people would take you seriously?

The apostle Paul was acutely discerning when he wrote that we need the armor of God to stand firm against the "schemes of the devil" and his "flaming arrows" (Eph. 6:11, 16, NASB). Paul went on to say in Corinthians that he didn't want himself or the Corinthians to be "outwitted by Satan; for we are not ignorant of his designs" (2 Cor. 2:11). Oh, this is a crucial scripture for our consideration. Paul is writing the Corinthian church in 2 Corinthians 2 about forgiveness for a brother who has sinned, been disciplined, and is now repentant. Paul wants them to forgive the person and not be too severe. He is in essence writing, let's get this thing, forgiveness, right because we know unforgiveness is one of Satan's schemes to put our love to the test and make us fail. The world needs to see that when a person sins, we can forgive and restore them. This is the kind of love we need today in the twenty-first century!

Metaphorically, it may be that Satan's sword is also double-edged (like God's sword, the Word), and he distributes it to all his demonic cohorts. Satanic forces use this weapon to propagate disunity in relationships and the Christian community. The enemy's weapons can stealthily gash friendships and shear spiritual bonds that have stood for decades. His sword is honed to its sharpest edge and can slash the feet from under the sturdiest believer. Repeated thrusting of this weapon creates a wound (offense) profound enough to separate blood-related Christian families.

The two sides of his blade? Vindication and vengeance.

Most of us have heard of the term *sinkholes*. A sinkhole is a depression in the ground that has no natural external surface drainage. Eventually, the subsurface cannot support the land above, and there is a sudden collapse. Precipitous, damaging, and sometimes life-threatening, everything is swallowed up. So it is when a Christian enters the trap of seeking vindication or when any one of us falls into the enemy's pit of vengeance. If we succumb to either of these practices, the enemy's blade creates an ingress into our hearts. It is only a matter of time before defensiveness, deterioration, and division will characterize our relationships.

Vindication

If a saint like St. Augustine of Hippo (in the quote above) could confess his struggle with the lust to vindicate himself, we shouldn't be surprised that the enemy can entice us to head down this dead-end road. The accuser of our soul is highly skilled in his temptations to lead us into the trap of vindication. Our ever-lurking pride and worldliness create the perfect storm of vulnerability to the enemy. And let's remember who we inherited this lust for vindication from in the first place: Adam and Eve. These two introduced to humanity the art of dodging sin by blaming others (Gen. 3:9-13).

> The LORD God called to the man and said to him, "Where are you?" He said, "I heard Your voice in the garden and was afraid because I was naked, so I hid myself." And He said, "Who told you that you were naked? Have you eaten from the tree of which I commanded you not to eat?" The man said, "The woman whom You gave to be with me, she gave me fruit of the tree, and I ate." Then the LORD God said to the woman, "What have you done?" And the woman said, "The serpent deceived me, and I ate."
>
> —Genesis 3:9-13

It seems so natural to fall into Satan's trap to think it is our responsibility to vindicate ourselves every time we are accused of almost anything. When the stakes are high, like our reputation at work or personal and spiritual integrity, we often succumb quickly. Satan whispers his lies in our ear, and we take the bait. The blame-shifting game is on.

We are not dealing with trivial issues here. A massive idol is at the heart of vindication—the idol of self. This idol needs regular feeding and polishing. When "self" rules, we will go to great lengths to preserve its standing. We will insanely engage in defending ourselves over ridiculous issues. If I don't defend myself, who will? If I don't convince others I have been misunderstood, who will? If I don't... If I don't...

If you work at a job with other people, you know firsthand how challenging it can be to not succumb to vindicating yourself when things don't go your way, or you are misunderstood. It is challenging to respond in some of these situations and not be defensive. Here are just a few examples.

- You came in thirty minutes late to an important staff meeting. You called to say you would be late, but you really did get stuck in traffic.

- When working on a collaborative project with a fellow employee, you do more than your part but can't compensate for the other person's failure. Your project goes down in flames.

- You are focused on a project with a looming deadline and in a hurry. Someone passes you in the hall and gives a hearty "good morning," but you don't respond. Later, you hear rumors from fellow employees about how unfriendly you are.

We need the Holy Spirit to remind us that the accuser of our soul is constantly, insidiously, at work to create discord in our relationships. I've written it before, but it merits repeating: The enemy strikes us at our weak points, not our strengths. The demons return time and again to whisper thoughts in our ears, let us overhear veiled gossip, or catch the slightest quips of other conversations—so easily misinterpreted. Like cluster bombs dropping on our path, we become disoriented and begin dodging personal responsibility, teachableness, and God's corrections. We have started the lifestyle of vindicating ourselves and not trusting God.

If we are injured by the thrusts of the enemy's sword of vindication, we may discover ourselves to be like a wounded animal. If you have ever tried to assist a wounded animal, you immediately remember the most challenging issue: The animal attempts to bite and lash out at anyone nearby. We are in deep trouble if we take the enemy's bait hook, line, and sinker and repeatedly attempt to vindicate ourselves. We predictably descend into the abyss of vindication, fighting fire with fire. In total defense mode, we strike at anyone who would dare to correct us, question our decision-making, or try to get us to assume responsibility for a mistake. We become unable to have meaningful conversations. Our relationships suffer, and we cannot enjoy fellowship with others. And unity? We are crippled and incapable.

Oh, what cost!

When we are stuck in the mode of lusting to be vindicated, the harmful byproducts are sobering and should be fearful. Our spiritual lives are at risk. We have allowed the enemy to steal from us the ability to forgive others. Read that previous sentence again—pause and read.

It is unconscionable that a person would say they are a follower of Christ and refuse to forgive. Yet you and I see Christians with broken relationships over unforgiveness almost everywhere we turn. Be brutally honest with yourself right now. Is this what you see when you look in the mirror?

How do you maintain a relationship with someone who always has to be right? It is challenging, if not impossible. Do you know a Christian brother or sister who forever tries to vindicate themselves when they make an error or when anything goes wrong that may reflect poorly on them?

I know the story of a person (in a Christian job setting) who was a division leader with great responsibility (let's call him John). John was talented, experienced, and discerning, yet he often told others how hardheaded he was. He was uncorrectable.

John performed admirably at 95 percent of his job. However, that other 5 percent was his Waterloo, his downfall. John appeared threatened when around other talented division leaders and constantly sought to vindicate himself. He always had to be correct and was quick to point out what he thought could go wrong with another person's suggestions.

The one lusting after vindication is deceived; repentance is out of their reach. Broken relationships will be their reward. If this is you, ask the Lord for the courage and strength to admit it. Cry out to the Holy Spirit for a spirit of repentance to fall on you right now.

There is a young man I have come across who will restore your faith in young people if you have any doubt that they can be zealous, humble, Bible-based in beliefs, and respectful of the opposite sex. Let's call him Sam. He is not perfect; yet Sam has made some excellent decisions that have primed him for spiritual success as he enters a dramatic professional path following college. This young man is on cue!

We were talking about humility recently, and Sam shared a story from his senior year in high school with his church youth group. He used this incident to explain how God had allowed him to choose humility. The boys' playfulness and foolishness got out of hand at summer camp with his church group, and the camp facilities were damaged. Sam did not participate in the actions that caused the damage. The young men apologized, took full responsibility for their actions, and made full amends. Sam sensed that the Lord directed him not to excuse or vindicate himself but to identify with the group in apologizing and making restitution. With maturity beyond his years, Sam saw that giving in to vindicating himself would shortcut an opportunity for the work of the Spirit in his life.

I've discovered that breaking the cycle of vindication allows me unlimited freedom from anxiety and inexhaustible joy. This is the heaviest of burdens to carry, the weight of pride so crystallized in your life that you must be correct, and no one is smart enough or mature enough to correct you. Preserving our pride, we are willing to lose friendships and loved ones. Proper rest can only come by laying down the affliction of such pride.

Where do you begin to deal with this lust for vindication if it is prevalent?

Hearken back to the beginnings of your spiritual life; you will remember the weight of sin taken off your shoulders when you were born again. If you are like me, your salvation experience was dramatic. I knew I needed a Savior; no one else could atone for my sins. Salvation meant that Jesus had paid the debts I could never pay. Jesus had shouldered all my shame, guilt, and humiliation. I was engrossed in this euphoric salvation yet simultaneously brought ever so low in abject humility. I felt the weight of Jesus' suffering for me.

Jesus gave His life for you. We are all in the same station of life. The ground is level at the foot of the cross. Every one of us was bound in sin, and it was addictive stuff. Jesus is the only one who can redeem us. "In Him we have redemption through His blood and the forgiveness of sins according to the riches of His grace" (Eph. 1:7). Together, every one of us who names Christ as Savior stands vindicated. The sobriety of this truth and its cost, the cross, will help us to squash the lustful desire of vindication.

What if we crucify the lust of vindication by making ourselves nothing? Paul gives us this simple instruction even a child can follow. "Therefore be imitators of God as beloved children. Walk in love, as Christ loved us and gave Himself for us as a fragrant offering and a sacrifice to God" (Eph. 5:1-2). Let us imitate Christ Himself.

Who, being in very nature God, did not consider equality with God something to be used to his own advantage; rather, he made himself nothing by taking the very nature of a servant, being made in human likeness.

—Philippians 2:6-7, NIV

Vengeance

Say the word *vengeance* to yourself right now and with gusto. What did it sound like to you? When I do that, it resounds with authority and terror. Authority if you are the one meting it out; terror if you recognize someone has made it their life's mission to pour it out on you. If you have received someone's vengeance, you understand how devious, loathsome, and shocking behavior can be.

When we fight fire with fire, an eye for an eye, we are not listening to the Holy Spirit but the evil spirit instead. If we seek vengeance, we have swallowed Satan's lure—we are hooked, hook, line, and sinker. And we will pay a significant cost: loss of peace and loss of our Christian witness, and we will inevitably teeter on the precipice of bitterness. Intimacy with God will wane and invariably vanish. Unity in my life with others will evaporate.

In seeking vengeance, we send a direct communique to God. I want to be in control. And I want vengeance now! Reader, don't tune me out now. We are zeroing in on the crucial issue of revenge. We have chosen to become the judge.

But stop the show. I thought God was the judge. Aha, there it is—we want to exact punishment and determine the penalty. We have lost our faith in God to do it. God has missed the boat; we know better. We have a more expedient timetable, and it is NOW! We are deceived and caught in Satan's web. When we operate in vengeance, we will miss participating in one of life's most challenging and rewarding experiences, offering forgiveness to someone who doesn't deserve it, someone just like us.

You must understand when it comes to vengeance that God doesn't leave any gray areas, ifs, ands, or buts. Vengeance belongs to Him. He will repay.

For we know him who said, "It is mine to avenge; I will repay," and again, "The Lord will judge his people."

—Hebrews 10:30, NIV

When we seek vengeance, we invariably get in God's way. And His justice may be delayed because of our impatience. God may not deliver justice, vengeance, or vindication tomorrow, next year, the next decade, or even in your lifetime. His vengeance is perfect, just, and right on time, nothing like ours.

You can be assured of this, dear saint: God is on the throne. In heaven, the truth will be known, and recompense will come. Eternity is a long, long time.

I have observed one other very significant issue surrounding vengeance. We often fail to consider that God's vengeance is righteous. His vengeance will support those who reside on the side of integrity. Don't expect vengeance to come if you are not on the side of truth. God doesn't play favorites.

We must be ever so careful; once initiated, vengeance can become a very emotional issue. You perceive someone has hurt you or your family and are livid. If you have gone down this path of revenge—leaving the Lord behind—your emotions will likely be at a fever pitch. And you may be blind to the consideration of decency, rationality, and sanity.

As head of a Christian school, I interacted with Christian parents over issues with their children. I once had a Christian parent sue me personally over a problem with the child not making an athletic team (I had no direct authority over picking individuals for the team). When everything was said and done, out in the open, and depositions completed, the parent had covertly gathered information by tape recording my and other's phone calls, which he initiated. It got even worse from there into the abyss of vengeance.

There is no more explicit portion in the New Testament regarding how we should get along as Christians than Romans 12:9-21. Concerning vindication and vengeance, this scripture is so critical I will include the entire section for your ease of reading. Please don't skim over these words. Pay close attention to phrases expressing how Paul expects us to treat one another and what he commands us to do.

> Love must be sincere. Hate what is evil; cling to what is good. Be devoted to one another in love. Honor one another above yourselves. Never be lacking in zeal, but keep your spiritual fervor, serving the Lord. Be joyful in hope, patient in affliction, faithful in prayer. Share with the Lord's people who are in need. Practice hospitality. Bless those who persecute you; bless and do not curse. Rejoice with those who rejoice; mourn with those who mourn. Live in harmony with one another. Do not be proud, but be willing to associate with people of low position. Do not be conceited. Do not repay anyone evil for evil. Be careful to do what is right in the eyes of everyone. If it is possible, as far as it depends on you, live at peace with everyone. Do not take revenge, my dear friends, but leave room for God's wrath, for it is written: "It is mine to avenge; I will repay," says the Lord. On the contrary: "If your enemy is hungry, feed him; if he is thirsty, give him something to drink. In doing this, you will heap burning coals on his head." Do not be overcome by evil, but overcome evil with good.
>
> —Romans 12:9-21

These verses have thirty-two commands; however, they all pivot on verse 9. Love must be sincere, without hypocrisy, no pretending. The love that Christ invites us to receive, His love, will not need to vindicate itself or seek vengeance. Through beholding Jesus, we can be free from the temptations of the enemy and the pressure of the world to embrace living in unforgiveness toward others. Forgiving others is not optional (Matt. 6:14-15); it is the standard set by Christ and expected of us. *The power of the blood of the Lamb and our testimony can overcome the greatest of personal injustices.* If this last sentence isn't true, then the gospel of Jesus is a fantasy. When God almighty was speaking to Abraham, He said rhetorically, "Is anything too difficult for the LORD?" (Gen. 18:14a).

Christ beckons us to be united with Him in the likeness of His death. "For if we have been united with Him in the likeness of His death, so shall we also be united with Him in the likeness of His resurrection" (Rom. 6:5).

And so it becomes the undeniable marker—the litmus test—of the child of God who has discovered the place of abiding in Christ and the place of immunity. That marker: to suffer wrong without vindicating oneself or seeking vengeance and trusting God for justice.

CHAPTER 10

MISSION POSSIBLE: FORGIVENESS AND RECONCILIATION IN FAMILIES

For *this* is the message that you heard from the beginning: We should love one another.

—1 John 3:11

Ruby

My mother's side of the family was separated from her brother's side for more than fifteen years because of offenses over the distribution of my Grandpa Milford's assets. It was all birthed from my mom being the executor of her dad's will. Misunderstanding and finger-pointing reached a fever pitch, and the enemy won; complete division ensued. And to boot, a considerable dose of vengeance was meted out on my immediate family (children).

The outcome was estrangement from my best-loved aunt and uncle, Buddy and Ruby. I was guilty by association. I looked up to my Uncle Buddy. I was a little boy when he was a Korean War hero and a guitar player, and he loved the Lord. I was mesmerized by him. He fought in a famous battle in the Korean War, Pork Chop Hill. Hundreds of US service members were killed, and the struggle was made into a major motion picture. Buddy was highly decorated and also wounded.

When I found out Buddy had died, I attended his funeral. No one on his side of the family would speak to me. If you have had a close family member ignore you and refuse to acknowledge or engage you, you can empathize with me. This degree of rejection is oh so painful. It is a deep feeling of estrangement and disappointment—all rolled into one mammoth gut punch. And Ruby? As a young teen, I spent time with Ruby and loved her. Over the next fifteen years, I somehow walled up that side of my life and heart and didn't think of them.

Tootling along, minding my own business, and believing I had resolved all the broken relationships in my life, I thought I was doing a darn good job at cleaning out the swampland of my rifts. One day, in quietness before the Lord, I heard a single word: Ruby. I wondered if she was even still alive. The short of it is that I found out she lived less than five miles from me. Finding her phone number was easy. I wrote a scripted text to speak from when I called her; if you know me, I also memorized it. I called and immediately lost my composure (I, the well-versed speaker who can dance with words on stage). Halting, searching for a word to spit out, it came, "Oh, Ruby, please forgive me; I should have made this call years ago."

There was total silence on the other end of the phone for at least five, six, or seven seconds, which seemed like five, six, or seven minutes. Like a blast of cool, refreshing air on one of Tulsa's 103-degree days with 84 percent humidity, her response came, "Oh, thank you, Timmy, for calling." I discovered that Ruby had cancer, and days later I took my granddaughter,

Cameron, with me, and we went to Ruby's house and prayed for her. I reconnected with her, and the reconciliation with her sons followed like a cascade of sparkling cold water over a bluff. Two years later, Ruby died.

A fantastic weight was lifted from my soul by reconciling with my mom's side of the family. I repented before the Lord. There were things I could have done differently and with more compassion and understanding.

Do you have any divisions in your family like mine? Ask yourself this question: Is this the way I want to continue my life, separated from my relatives? What keeps you from beginning the healing process with whatever person this is? For far too many of us, the hangup is our pride.

Pride has a way of constantly seeping into the agonizing experiences of our lives. "I'm not the guilty one" somehow numbs the heartbreak. We can say those words so effortlessly and as a result suffer the loss of loved ones for the sake of our foolish pride. And there comes the cold war, with few conversations or discussions other than sports or the weather. We have participated in the ruin of fellowship in return for a paper-thin truce. We begrudgingly tolerate each other. Perhaps we pledge to each other to discuss only those things that have little significance for the bettering of our souls. Or we lay out land mines and threaten others that we will explode if they so much as raise the forbidden subject of my mistakes, errors, or sin.

When Peter asked Jesus if he should forgive his brother as many as seven times, Jesus responded with a parable about the kingdom of heaven (Matt. 18:23-27). Jesus compared God's kingdom to a king with a servant who owed him a thousand talents (well over a billion dollars in today's money). Jesus said the king ordered that the servant with his wife and children to be sold to make payment. The servant's dramatically poor choices resulted in such a state (an unrepayable debt), creating havoc for the entire family. But it is notable and imperative that we see the servant found mercy when he humbled himself. It is the same with our family relationships; if we desire unity, there is no place for pride. Humility will win the day.

The Front Lines of the War

Family relationships, all family relationships, are under attack today. The nuclear family, huh? Who needs it! That hard-to-get-along-with brother, aunt, or grandparent? They don't exist to me; I will erase them from my consciousness.

Let's confess the obvious: Family relationships can be the most challenging arena for people to manage. Phone calls, birthdays, family get-togethers, and almost any interaction can be a painful reminder of offenses and unforgiveness.

But shouldn't it be different with Christian families?

We have an enemy, and he is scheming, insidious, and treacherous. He gives no quarter; he is always on the prowl. There is one author of confusion and division, and it is the enemy of your soul, the devil. The battlefront the enemy has staged in full force is the family. We must cast ourselves upon the Holy Spirit for discernment and strength to fight with the sword of the Spirit and Spirit-empowered prayer.

The war is raging, yet many Christians casually saunter to church on Sunday, sing a few songs, hear a sermon, and check the Christian boxes. They are what I categorize as functional Christians. Some of them may give their best shot at getting with the program. They attend the monthly Bible study. They give to the missions program and tithe. They may even show up for the church junior high car wash. But they continue to hold a grudge against that snarky brother-in-law, or they shame their brother for his second divorce. And that nephew who can't keep a job, they are merciless in their criticism. Do I need to say more?

Fellow readers, so much more is happening in the spirit realm with the world forces of this darkness and the spiritual forces of wickedness in the heavenly places. We must recognize that our struggle and battle are not against flesh and blood. Our prickly, provoking relative is not the enemy!

The Triggers

There are so many different triggers for division in Christian families: lifestyles, American or foreign car, vegetarianism, questionable church affiliation, and on and on. The opportunities for division are endless. Don't get me started on money. Little things, seemingly insignificant, can turn out to be big deals. Do you go to public or private schools? You homeschool? What are you thinking? We go to the first service because we are more passionate about Jesus. You eat sushi!? And then, one of the most critical factors possible is, "Do you go to church on the real sabbath, Saturday?" There he goes again, judging me for supporting *that* president.

When we are experiencing our last moments of life, how many of us will remember the president our brother voted for? Yet so many family members refuse to entertain forgiveness over political choices. How heartbreaking.

In Luke 16:8, Jesus gives a parable about an unjust steward. "The master commended the dishonest steward, because he had acted prudently. For the sons of this world are wiser in their own generation than the sons of light." In the parable, Jesus is pointing out that those who are unsaved and living in the world act wiser or truer to their principles and standards than those in the kingdom of God to their principles and standards. Those in the world are often shrewder in their financial investing than Christians are in investing in the lives of people with eternal value. We too frequently fail to recognize how crucial it is to have harmony with our relatives and the powerful witness of a healthy Christian family.

Rod Nordland, an acknowledged non-believer and former war correspondent for *The New York Times* and *Newsweek*, has faced death many times in warzones and escaped. Rod now faces an adversary he can't dodge: the most lethal form of brain tumor, glioblastoma. When asked in an interview what he is doing to prepare for his imminent death, Rod said, "I'm repairing my relationships more than anything else."[1] This man of the world facing death recognizes where he should be with others: with repaired relationships. We, the followers of the Prince of Peace, should be so wise.

We must discover that none of these inane concerns we let divide our families are the real issue. The issue is the love of Christ. For Christ's sake and the kingdom of heaven, we must let love penetrate our first, most crucial mission field: our family unit and extended family.

Let me address one harrowing topic that touches almost every family line today. Its invasion of the family raises untold issues, conflicts, and separation, leaving many unanswered, conceivably unanswerable questions: a son or daughter, a granddaughter or grandson, a first cousin, or practically any relative involved with, dating, or married to someone of the same sex. There, I've said it!

Everyone has an opinion on the topic of same-sex attraction, dating, or marriage.

It would be implausible to suggest that Jesus or Paul affirmed anything but the conventional female and male relationships when it comes to sex and marriage. Nevertheless, the issue goes so much further and deeper in our culture. After all, our government has sanctioned gay marriage and protects it with laws. The entire gay culture is now recognized and celebrated everywhere, from entertainment to many mainstream denominations.

Jesus loves everyone, and His followers should do the same. Whether it is a son who has married his male partner or a granddaughter living with her female lover, our instruction from the Word of God is crystal clear. Do everything you can to be at peace with all your family and relatives. "If it is possible, as far as it depends on you, live at peace with everyone" (Rom. 12:18, NIV). We are compelled to make every attempt to let the love of Christ through us attract our wayward kin into the kingdom of God; here, they can discover acceptance, forgiveness, cleansing from sin, healing, restoration, and righteousness. All things indeed are possible in Christ, all things.

In my interactions with Christians, I have seen the gamut of reactions to the thorny issue of same-sex attraction. It is difficult to fathom the pain of the Christian couple whose children all attend Christian schools K-12 and then Christian colleges. Then it happens: Their child announces the choice to be gay by posting a picture on social media with their same-sex partner. These parents choose to maintain lines of open communication, and their love and concern give them repeated opportunities for a godly voice in their child's life. And I have witnessed the polar-opposite reactions from parents.

Please listen to my heart as I write. I am not lobbying for accepting the sinful actions of children or any other family members. I'm lobbying to keep faith alive and believe we can play a part in the healing and restoration of our kinsfolk.

Love Will Win

John is often recognized as the disciple of love. Six times in the epistles of John he refers to himself as the one whom Jesus loved (John 13:23; 19:26; 20:2; 21:7, 21:20, and 21:24). John goes on to mention the word *love* forty-three times in these three short letters, John 1, 2, and 3. But John doesn't present a mere treatise on love; instead, He presents Jesus and the incarnation of love. His love of Christ was so much more than an abstract belief. John understood that the embodiment of the love of God became flesh in Jesus Christ.

John's presentation of the love of Christ brings Christ's love to life. This love has eyes, feet, and hands. Herein lies one of the most significant tests a Christian will ever confront: Christ desires His love to be seen through us to *all* others. We are to be His eyes, feet, and hands. Take that little word, *all*, and apply it to your relatives, not just some, but all. Try on for size some of the synonyms of the word *all* and direct them to your family:

complete, entire, everyone, every single one. Yes, even the one married to his male partner.

Well, who am I to talk about this? Go ahead, point your finger at me this very moment and scream, "You don't understand the suffering and destruction *that* family member caused in my life." Maybe you can't give me sway into your present situation with family; it makes no difference. These words I am about to write embody one of the glorious truths about the love of Christ. And it applies to every follower of Jesus.

> There is not a single broken relationship that His love cannot succor. And if both parties embrace the love of Christ, reconciliation is the natural, spiritual outcome.

If we are not being led by the love of Christ with the discernment of the Holy Spirit, the possibility of unity in the family exponentially decreases. To muddle matters, none of us have attained a state of perfection (we continue to sin). Our sins seemingly keep the attainment of peace, togetherness, and communication in our family structure just beyond our grasp. In Psalm 51:4, David clarifies that our sins are ultimately against the Lord and Him only. But this doesn't mean our sins only affect our relationship with God. Far be it; we know that none of us sin in a vacuum and that our sins affect other people, especially those close to us, family. In most families, a broken relationship between two family members can bleed into the dynamics of the entire family structure.

Love covers; it doesn't cover up.

Love does cover. One of the unsearchable abysses of God's love is the endless grace to cover other's sins and extend forgiveness in exchange. We must have this ineffable grace operating in our lives to entertain forgiveness over devastating family disputes and painful hurts. It extends an impenetrable blanket of peace. That covering of love gives the offended, hurt party the strength and courage to put the events to rest. When the love of

Christ is in operation and forgiveness is applied, this majestic love enables parties to keep the events under the blood of Jesus once they have been thoroughly addressed. When events are covered with the blood of Jesus, they will no longer be shared with parties who are not part of the problem or the solution to the problem. Love covers. Love has no boundaries for its ability to cover every imaginable offense (the son who finds out at the end of his mother's life that he was not his father's son but the product of an affair his mom had while married to his thought-to-be dad). Can the love of Christ cover even this? Oh, yes!

Love covers is simple to understand: the opposite of covering is to uncover. When we choose to cover a family member's failures, we display before the throne of heaven the authenticity of our love for that person. In family dynamics, we often know secrets about each other that no one can access. Love does not repeat those matters to anyone.

But love does not cover up. Love will be willing to take the time to truly listen to someone who has been hurt and humbly admit errors. Love does not push hurts and offenses under the carpet and just hopes they will magically disappear with time. Love does not look for quick fixes so we can get on the road to the next thing; it is not in a hurry. Love is patient and courageous.

Yes, love is patient. Love lives in reality, not denial. And few things will tax your patience as dealing with mental health issues in a spouse, son, daughter, or close relative. I've watched it firsthand and seen the destruction, literally. The loss, financially (through gambling addiction). The emotional carnage (through abuse). The lifelong attention (demanded) to severe schizophrenia. It can be brutal.

In the early church of the second and third centuries, patience was the first virtue written about as a comprehensive treatise by three prominent Christian writers. "The early Christians believed that God is patient and that Jesus visibly embodied patience."[2] These early followers of Jesus lived in a world that was out of control. They envisioned patience as the first virtue to practice to live in this world and practically display the love of Christ. We are no different today. And few other challenges can be as demanding as living and sharing the love of Christ with relatives who suffer from mental or emotional illness. Is God's love patient and sufficient? Praise God; yes, it is!

What's a Person to Do?

How does God want us to act when the differences lead to a seemingly insurmountable dispute?

One person thinks they have the Word of the Lord on a subject, and that is the end of it. But the other party believes they are walking in the truth. Instead of suggesting a few traditional answers like mediation, counseling, or compromise, let me offer what I believe is God's first choice as a pathway for peace in family disagreements.

What if we turned the table on family clashes, disputes, and fractures? What if we made the issue a question of each person's commitment and relationship to Jesus? The parties involved would have to answer some grave questions before God.

> For not one of us lives for himself, and not one dies for himself; for if we live, we live for the Lord, or if we die, we die for the Lord; therefore whether we live or die, we are the Lord's.

—Romans 14:7-8, NASB

I believe that if disagreeing family members came before the Lord Jesus Christ, in all humility, they would recognize that their disputes are more about their brokenness. If we bow down before the Lord and ask Him to open our eyes to our conflicts, we will likely discover that our divergent thoughts are often over items that make little difference in the totality of life. Defensiveness, criticism, and gossip would be laid bare. And judgments would be exposed.

There is one Judge, and we are not that person.

Furthermore, in these instances of division between Christian family members and the discussion about what is essential, the mature Christian must ask the inevitable question: Am I acting in love, or am I being selfish? Is my interpretation of an incident, my judgment of someone's actions, or my conviction harming a relationship or someone personally? These are deep waters to ford. But it is time for you and me to head upstream.

We become so concerned about who is right and wrong that we forget it's not about who is right and who is wrong. It's about my relationship with Jesus. Can I defer to others and recognize when exercising my freedoms causes a person to stumble? Am I willing to examine my life next to the Word of God on issues?

No one said forgiveness or reconciliation in families would be simple. It is hard. Yielding to the Spirit may look like small steps, one after another. A sibling or parent's injuries can be brutal, and the damage can be indescribable. Yet there is hope if we do yield to the Spirit of God. If we don't, the long-term results may be excruciating.

I know Christians who have repeatedly turned away from overtures of reconciliation from an abusive parent or sibling who is now following Christ. Then the worst of all news comes. While the recipient of abuse ponders extending forgiveness, the offending party passes away. Forgiveness and reconciliation will take place in heaven. However, this is not God's best or intended outcome. Christ glories in His love, facilitating forgiveness and reconciliation on this side of heaven.

Reconciliation with family members begins with one person: *you*. But it will never happen until *you* take the time to listen to the other person's story. There may be legitimate issues you must empathize with. All these thoughts butt up against the question with the force of a fast-moving train: How serious are you about reuniting with family members you are steadfastly separated from? There is that irritating mother-in-law, the overbearing uncle, or the deceitful niece. But, dear reader, God provides no hint of any exceptions to His healing love.

The way of forgiveness leaves no options for unforgiveness. You must be willing to assume your part in the division and seek forgiveness, whether your responsibility is 2 percent or 90 percent. The Holy Spirit will lead you into all truth.

Oh, How Deep the Offense!

Offenses, hurt, pain, sexual abuse, manipulation, and the myriad violations of one's soul by a family member seem impossible to resolve. Consider the indescribable: a relative who cheats in marriage with your wife! Many of you have experienced the rejection of a father or mother. Yet I declare to you the very words of Jesus in His High Priestly prayer, "My prayer is not for them alone. I pray also for those who will believe in me through their message, that all of them may be one, Father, just as you are in me and I am in you. May they also be in us so that the world may believe that you have sent me" (John 17:20-21). Jesus' prayer to the Father is pointedly clear: Our relationships with our family members—all family members—should emulate that of the Father and Son. With God, all things are possible.

God has given us the strength and courage to seek reconciliation in family relationships. God has given us the best helper for this job, the Holy Spirit. There is no higher or more wonderful gift than the Holy Spirit of God.

People are watching; the world is watching. What do they see when they look at your family? Does your family cause others to believe in Christ and His message of love and unity? Or do they see it as another confirmation that this Christian stuff sounds good, but who lives a life inculcated with its beliefs? Or, put more penetratingly in the words of Mahatma Gandhi, "If it weren't for Christians, I'd be a Christian."[3]

But what about you? How would people in your family line describe you? Are you kind and forgiving, or do you keep a precise record of offenses and hurts? Are you gentle and understanding with others or quarreling, proud, and selfish?

I know very few Christians who would turn down the offer of Christ's peace in their family. Do you have peace with your family and extended family? It matters to Christ, and it should matter to you.

Saint Columba (d: 597) was an Irish abbot and missionary credited with spreading Christianity across what is now Scotland. He was responsible for founding the abbey on Iona, where Saint Aidan of Lindisfarne lived as a monk. Remarkable miracles marked his life. His spiritual reach extends even into today.

On his deathbed, Saint Columba said, "I give to you, my children, these final words: 'Be at peace with one another, bound together by mutual and unfeigned love. If you do this, according to the example of the ancient fathers, God, who gives strength to the righteous, will bless you, and I, abiding with Him, shall intercede for you. Not only will God provide all things needed for this present life, but He shall prepare for you the blessings of eternity."[4]

God's Word is replete with this plea from beginning to end: God desires unity in the family. It is up to you to humble yourself and respond to His call.

"Be completely humble and gentle; be patient, bearing with one another in love. Make every effort to keep the unity of the Spirit through the bond of peace" (Eph. 4:2-3, NIV).

The Ultimate Invitation

Walking in the light of Christ resoundingly opposes the life of the flesh. This is the stark contrast between the kingdom of God and the world forces of this present darkness. It is stunning that Paul, in Galatians 5:19-23, lists the works of the flesh that are so clearly evident and in opposition to the fruit of the Spirit. And he includes in this nefarious list things such as sorcery, orgies, *rivalries, dissensions*, and *divisions*.

Fellow Christians, Christ invites us to walk in His light. "But if we walk in the Light as He Himself is in the Light, we have fellowship with one another, and the blood of Jesus His Son cleanses us from all sin" (1 John 1:7, NASB). If we walk in His light, we will grow up as His followers into maturity. To be mature followers of Jesus means to be mature in fellowship with Him and one another. What is your capacity for fellowship with your relatives?

We cannot escape this truth: Your relationship with your family and all other followers of Jesus is an undeniable indicator of your maturity in Christ.

It is up to you to take the next steps for reconciliation in your family. The Holy Spirit supplies the power; He only needs a willing heart. Will you open your ears to hear His Word and your heart to do His will?

CHAPTER 11

THE TWIN DEMONS OF DESTRUCTION: GOSSIP AND BETRAYAL

The devil is the great gossip. He is always saying bad things about others because he is the liar who tries to split the church.[1]

—POPE ST. FRANCES

I'd like to promise them they won't be betrayed, but I can't. Eventually we all go under that knife.[2]

—IAN MORGAN CRON and SUZANNE STABILE

Pope Francis has a pet peeve, and it is gossip. He pronounced a profound metaphor about gossip when he called it worse than the coronavirus.[3] The pope often forewarns about the ills of gossiping. The pope, Billy Graham, St. Paul, and most meaningfully, Jesus Christ our Lord, rail against gossip and recognize its demonic, destructive power.

Billy Graham stated it as bluntly as he could: "But I do know this: Gossiping can be one of the most destructive and cruelest habits any person can practice. It destroys the reputation of others because it's often based on half-truths or outright lies. It also destroys the character of the person who gossips; who is going to trust you as a friend if you have a reputation as a gossip? No wonder the Bible says, 'A perverse man stirs up conflict, and a gossip separates close friends' (Proverbs 16:28, NIV)."[4] A person who gossips is identified in the same sentence as a perverse man. Wow! Meditate for a moment on some synonyms of gossip: dirt, intimidation, scandal, and betrayer.

Jesus drove a stake into the heart of gossip when He said, "I tell you, on the day of judgment people will give account for every careless word they speak, for by your words you will be justified, and by your words you will be condemned" (Matt. 12:36-37, ESV). This scripture should give us pause as we cringe at remembering the imprudence of our words about others. Our words are eternally recorded; the day will come when they either justify or condemn us.

> Therefore, whatever you have said in the dark shall be heard in the light, and what you have whispered in private rooms shall be proclaimed on the housetops.
>
> —Luke 12:3, ESV

Where is the dark Jesus speaks of in Luke 12:3? It is the secret things said about others in clandestine conversations. It is when we whisper about a person's failures to someone. It happens daily to believer after believer over cell phones, our private text messages, the blind carbon copy of that email, and at the coffee shop where we meet for devotions.

Few things in life demolish fellowship, divide friends, and devastate families like gossip. I've officially labeled *gossip* as the most wicked of all words. The word itself reeks of a salacious invitation to please your flesh. As unsavory as gossip is, there is still something alluring about it to our soul. Gossip can titillate our emotions, stir our minds, and render our will powerless. If we are not walking in the Spirit, we will walk into conversations littered with gossip. We may be the ones unknowingly starting those conversations.

Let's get a handle on what gossip is.

This is my working definition of gossip: sharing information or a problem with someone about a third party, and the person you are sharing it with has no need to know the information. It is that subtle drop in a conversation when someone shares, "Oh, did you know the new employee in our department has been married three times?" The news spreads about the new teacher at your child's school: "I think this is her fourth school to work at in four years; there must be something wrong with her."

One reason gossip is so proliferated is its acceptance in our culture. The culture loves gossip! From gossip magazines and the paparazzi industry to blogs and political news, it's challenging to turn off the gossip firehose. However, gossip gets much closer home to us than movie stars, political figures, and elite athletes. Gossip assaults us with words about the worship pastor, our friends, coworkers, and the janitor at school. Everyone is a potential candidate for the enemy's cruelest words: *gossip* and the destruction it breeds.

Gossip is the forte of the enemy; he utilizes it to destroy the fellowship and unity we long for and work for in the body of Christ. The Word of God is congruent throughout the breadth of scriptures concerning this dastardly word, *gossip*, and the deeds it initiates. These particular scriptures below should be fearfully sobering. And we need to get this right; godly fear is the appropriate response to God's Word when it directly addresses how we live the Christian life. "These are the ones I look on with favor: those who are humble and contrite in spirit, who tremble at my word" (Isa. 66:2b, NIV).

Read these Words slowly and with a heart open to their gravity.

- "Do not go about spreading slander among your people. 'Do not do anything that endangers your neighbor's life. I am the LORD'" (Lev. 19:16, NIV).

- "Whoever secretly slanders his neighbor, him I will destroy; no one who has a haughty look and an arrogant heart will I endure" (Ps. 101:5, NASB).

- "The lips of fools bring them strife, and their mouths invite a beating" (Prov. 18:6, NIV).

- "And just as they did not see fit to acknowledge God, God gave them up to a depraved mind, to do those things that are not proper, *people* having been filled with all unrighteousness, wickedness, greed, and evil; full of envy, murder, strife, deceit, and malice; *they are* gossips, and although they know the ordinance of God, that those who practice such things are worthy of death, they not only do the same, but also approve of those who practice them (Rom. 1:28-29, 32, NASB).

These inspired words of God raise two crucial questions.

1. How do we shield our hearts from receiving gossip?

2. And how do we rid our hearts of the sinful propensity to gossip?

1. How do we shield our hearts from receiving gossip?

What I am about to pen is a hard word, but it is not my word; it is the Word of God. The most effective defense against gossip is choosing not to be around someone with a penchant for gossip. Ouch! I understand it is dramatic and seemingly judgmental, but gossip is a slippery slope. It subtly hooks you and draws you down into its crevices.

As I have talked with people about gossip, I've discovered from others—and had to admit it to myself—that we have a penchant for gossiping with our closest friends. The guardrails are down, and we say things we wouldn't usually share with others. I've asked myself, "Why did I gossip with close friends?" The conclusion was obvious: I felt safe because of the assumed confidentiality with a close friend. *But the Spirit of the Lord jumped all over this thought, and He shouted to me, "This is still gossip, and it is destructive to your soul!"*

That person—you may call a friend—who repeatedly shares gossip with you is not a relationship that is helpful to your life in Christ. You should be candid with them and let them know that the Lord is putting His finger on gossip in your life. Be frank: You may need to humble yourself and confess to them that you have willingly participated in gossip with them and ask their forgiveness. Don't point the blame at them; assume responsibility for your actions. If gossip persists in this relationship, you must do precisely what the Word of God instructs you: Get away from that person. Something magnetic can occur in your soul with a friendship that shares gossip: The gossip a friend shares with you may pull gossip out of you.

> One who goes about as a slanderer reveals secrets; therefore do not associate with a gossip.
>
> —Proverbs 20:19, NASB

You may have made a conscious decision to observe your words carefully and do your best not to participate in gossip. Yet sometimes you are trapped in a situation where someone shares gossip. Rather than remove yourself immediately, you endure the situation thinking you don't want to embarrass anyone and are mature enough to weather a little gossip. *Wrong!* If you listen to gossip, it will influence you. This is the destructive power of gossip, absorbed quickly into our innermost being. And it will stick to your soul and spirit.

I had to pray earnestly for years to get victory over a fiery piece of gossip shared with me over three decades ago about someone I worked with. Its lingering residue lay dormant in my soul. At random times, the thought of that gossip would raise its head indiscriminately when I was around locations that reminded me of them, saw something about the person online, or showed up at the same event. Approximately twenty-five years later, I was thrust into connecting with this person professionally. It was a fantastic challenge not to let the gossip I had listened to decades ago affect my attitude toward the person. I am now freed from this gossip only by the power of the Holy Spirit. And I have committed to engage kindly whenever I see that person. While gaining freedom from that gossip, I discovered a powerful and ruthless truth about gossip.

The gossip you listen to about a person may color your mindset of them for years, if not decades, to come.

Gossip is enticing; its allure numbs you. Once its hook is in your flesh, it reels you in effortlessly. The more salacious the gossip, the more seducing it becomes. Here's the unsurpassed wickedness of gossip; it takes just a tiny morsel to accomplish its filthy deed.

The words of a gossiper are like dainty morsels, and they go down into the innermost parts of the body.

—Proverbs 18:8, NASB

You can shield yourself from gossip by employing the whole armor of God (Eph. 6:10-18). In this scripture, we are instructed to gird our loins with the truth, put on the breastplate of righteousness, shoe our feet with the gospel, take up the shield of faith to extinguish all the flaming missiles of the evil one, take the helmet of salvation and the sword of the Spirit, and employ Spirit-empowered prayer. All parts of this armor hinge on recognizing the truth first. Gossip is evil; we need to call it for what it is and get away from it quickly anytime it infringes on our walk with Christ.

2. How do we rid our hearts of the sinful propensity to gossip?

All lasting change in our lives begins in one action: vulnerability. I laughingly confess that the Christian life would not be so difficult save for one particularly troubling scripture: "Therefore confess your sins to each other and pray for each other so that you may be healed. The prayer of a righteous person is powerful and effective" (Jas. 5:16, NIV).

The truth is we must speak honestly to someone about our sins, and yes, that includes the humbling, embarrassing practice of gossiping or listening to gossip. I wish I could build a sound argument for just confessing my sins to the Lord. This may be true at times; however, the preponderance of Scripture is clear: I must be honest about my sin with the ones God knits me with (Eph. 4:25; Col. 3:9). The gossip I listen to, or my penchant to gossip, is sinful. I need to own it and repent.

Reader, serious consequences come from being outed as a gossip or being caught red-handed repeating gossip. I have seen it many times; it is not pretty. Being found guilty and facing gossip from a supervisor, pastor, or group of friends is disorienting. Sadly, I rarely see a person caught in gossip embrace humility and brokenness and own up to their failure—excuses abound.

When it comes to participating in gossip, the choices you make, time after time, will turn into habits. These habits will inevitably turn into strongholds. The Word of God creates guardrails for us about gossip that help us avoid it, leading to a peaceful life and fruitfulness as a child of God.

There is a sober warning in Proverbs, "Like a city that is broken into and without walls so is a person who has no self-control over his spirit" (Prov. 25:28, NASB). Throughout the Old and New Testaments, gossip is assailed as evil and destructive to our spiritual life. But many Christians pick and choose what they submit to their life in Christ. And in so doing, they deceive themselves into believing a little gossip here and there is not that harmful.

- I'm just trying to console my friend by listening to all her hurts from that dastardly associate pastor.

- We parents have a right to know everything about our teacher's personal history. And, oh, do people love to share it with others.

- I need to know that person's history so I can pray for them rightly.

If you want to shut the door on gossip and your susceptibility to it, you must choose the boundaries God has established in His Word. Suppose you think something concerning gossip falls in the gray area. In that case, the Holy Spirit is likely warning you that you have entered the enemy's most infectious, diseased territory.

"Lord, you alone are my portion and my cup; you make my lot secure. The boundary lines have fallen for me in pleasant places; surely I have a delightful inheritance" (Ps. 16:5-6, niv).

Betrayal

> It has been said that it is impossible to forgive a man who deliberately hurts you for the sole purpose of destroying you or lowering you. If this be true, you have but one hope: to see this unfair hurt as coming by permission from God for the purpose of lifting your stature above that place where formerly you stood.[5]
>
> —Gene Edwards, *The Prisoner in the Third Cell*

There are many kinds of trauma in life that invade and destroy relationships. But few events match betrayal. It can come from a Christian brother, sister, friend, or even a close relative—making it even more dastardly. Can it get any worse than this?

A betrayal from a close relative that happens at an early age may limit our capacity and desire for closeness to others for years to come. When any of this comes your way, the pain and devastation may traverse directly to the depths of your soul.

A Snapshot of the Betrayer

A betrayer is motivated by selfishness. Simply put, his gain is worth more than the other's loss. He may gain emotional support from others, financial advance, or bolster his reputation, but it is always at another's expense.

A betrayer can completely disregard relationships and how his actions impact others. Ah, this is where the enemy entices so many. He blinds the perpetrator to the deadly dominos that will follow his fallacious behavior.

A betrayer does not see the "big picture" impact of what his betrayal could cost his family. The rub with deception is that you are deceived. You see down a tiny tunnel. Everyone around you can testify the sky is blue, but you are convinced it is orange. Your compass grows smaller and smaller until it only reaches out to see how you can gain from another's loss.

A betrayer does not see how his actions have transgressed the most basic rules for civility and behavior. Kindness has been exchanged for rudeness, decorum for indecency, and decency for dishonesty.

A betrayer's actions have the most damaging impact when they betray someone they have had a relationship with.

Destructive forces are at work in the city; threats and lies never leave its streets. If an enemy were insulting me, I could endure it; if a foe were rising against me, I could hide. But it is you, a man like myself, my companion, my close friend, with whom I once enjoyed sweet fellowship at the house of God, as we walked about among the worshipers. My companion attacks his friends; he violates his covenant.

—Psalm 55:11-14, 20, NIV

If the betrayer's actions become public, he will lose his reputation with many people. Even if the betrayer repents and truly owns his actions, still what people may think of when his name is mentioned is that hurtful behavior. This nagging question may haunt him, "Was my gain worth the loss of my reputation and relationships?"

The one who betrays a spouse in marriage or a deep-hearted friend has moved into an even more profound level of self-deception. They may excuse their actions based on the other person's shortcomings. Still, they violate one of these decisive pronouncements in Scripture about love. "It does not act disgracefully, it does not seek its own benefit; it is not provoked, does not keep an account of a wrong suffered" (1 Cor. 13:5, NASB).

It has been my experience that the person who betrays a brother or sister in the Lord is often won over by the world's standards, thus justifying his action. There is that classic line I have heard from more than one person who betrayed a Christian in financial dealings: "You just don't understand; it's different in business."

To the Betrayed

Gene Edwards (in the quote above) puts betrayal in its proper place. It can be one of God's most extraordinary graces in our lives and brings us in touch with His majesty and commitment to our eventual holiness. Many of you can attest to the astounding life lessons and step up in faith resulting from sinister betrayals. The most profound lesson I learned from betrayal was God's challenge not to repeat the betrayals I encountered to others. I have experienced the glory of God in learning how to cover a brother's sins.

Have you had a personal experience with betrayal? I pray not, but as I journey through life, I am surprised at the number of us—so many more than I anticipated—who have had this encounter with the wickedest of the dark side.

I was going to write about a few of my nastiest, most heartbreaking betrayals, but then I realized something. Your betrayals are every bit as brutal and devastating as mine. To those of us who have wallowed in the mire and stench, the fog and wanderings of betrayal, reminding ourselves of the experience is like sloshing around old vomit in our mouths. Here are a few examples of betrayal my friends have grappled with.

- That once-in-a-lifetime business deal ensured financial security for life and an inheritance for his children, and his employee betrayed him.

- He convinced himself to expose a friend's homosexual struggles to the church leadership after the friend had shared those struggles with him in confidence.

- A young man bailed in a relationship with a girl he had gotten pregnant (after all, they weren't married yet).

- A daughter who is unforgiving of a parent's mistakes takes it out on them by withholding a relationship with the grandkids.

You can extend forgiveness to the one who has betrayed you by God's grace. I realize the offering of forgiveness seems scandalous to our natural inclinations. The raw pain from being betrayed does not heal quickly; it is not easily moved on from. The betrayal from a loved one may require you to take trip after trip to the feet of Jesus and cry out for the strength to forgive. However, if you are the recipient of this reprehensible act, please consider this counterintuitive, outrageous advice: The person who betrayed you does not need to know you have forgiven them. I pray that statement doesn't make you scream out with anger. However, in the extension of forgiveness, you are set free from the prison of unforgiveness.

There is profound closure that comes with betrayal when the one who harmed you asks for forgiveness. But this dramatic step is a work of the

Holy Spirit in the betrayer's life. God has the grace for a person who has been betrayed to forgive.

In offering forgiveness to your betrayer, you share the sufferings and humility of Christ. The late singer-songwriter Jane Marczweski—known professionally as Nightbirde—said, "If you can't see Him, look lower."[6] She discovered Christ on the bathroom floor, a private, graphic place of lowliness. In this place of brokenness and humility, no opinion matters save that of our Lord and Savior, Christ Jesus.

There is a richness of intimacy to be found in Jesus when you take the extreme step of forgiving your betrayer. Take advantage of this costly and rare spiritual opportunity.

> My brothers, count it all joy when you fall into diverse temptations, knowing that the trying of your faith develops patience. But let patience perfect its work, that you may be perfect and complete, lacking nothing.
>
> —James 1:2-4

To the Betrayer

Let me be frank. We all have had a little *Judas* (the ultimate betrayer) in us. In a moment of sincere honesty and openness, most of us would confess to having betrayed someone.

As a personal observation—which I have found to be consistent with other people's betrayal experiences—those caught in the Judas Iscariot role find repentance challenging to embrace. The trait that often stalls repentance in its tracks is pride. Being uncovered as a betrayer dramatically attacks one's persona and reputation. Pride takes a direct hit as if from a ballistic missile. It is all a bit too much for a very proud person.

Another reason that forestalls repentance for the betrayer is that repentance may require considerable restitution. Restitution seldom seems to be considered or discussed in concert with repentance, though it should be a tangible, necessary consideration. Should restitution need to be made, the cost of repentance becomes a living reality. Restitution can come in many forms besides monetary action. It can be multiple asks for forgiveness that need to be made. It could lead to previous acts of betrayal being brought to light and needing to be addressed.

A friend of mine (let's call him Marcus) came to the Lord during the Jesus Movement days in his early twenties. Before he came to know Christ, Marcus had worked in a store, seemingly serving faithfully. The small store owner thought Marcus to be one of his best employees. The owner had no idea Marcus was stealing small amounts of money, which added up to a substantial sum. In one of his most humiliating and humbling acts, Marcus returned to the store where he no longer worked, admitted the thefts, and paid back every dollar. He pursued other acts of restitution that the Holy Spirit brought to his mind.

M. Basilea Schlink said, "True repentance is marked by a desire to make amends. If we are genuinely sorry, we will want to bless those we have grieved or harmed and do all the good in our power."[7]

The Christian brother or sister who betrays another Christian has this fact in their favor. The forgiveness of God's compass reaches the very outskirts of our imagination and then infinitely farther.

> Brothers *and sisters*, even if a person is caught in any wrongdoing, you who are spiritual are to restore such a person in a spirit of gentleness; each one looking to yourself so that you are not tempted as well. Bear one another's burdens, and thereby fulfill the law of Christ.
>
> —Galatians 6:1-2, NASB

There is hope for healing from betrayal, gossip, and disloyalty. Whether we are the recipients or the perpetrators, there is hope for achieving a clean heart.

No matter the degree of injustice. No matter if the actions appear to be from the devil himself. When we face these juggernauts of life—gossip and betrayal—God can work them for good in us as we take up our cross and follow Him. There is no place for confusion on this topic. God does not bring these evils into our lives, but oh, can He redeem them for our best.

I love the hope this scripture instills. "Come back to the place of safety, all you prisoners who still have hope! I promise this very day that I will repay two blessings for each of your troubles" (Zech. 9:12, NLT).

CHAPTER 12

THE X-FACTORS

The X factor: "A variable in a given situation that could have the most impact on the outcome."[1]

A Christian fellowship lives and exists by the intercession of its members for one another, or it collapses. I can no longer condemn or hate a brother for whom I pray, no matter how much trouble he causes me.[2]

—DIETRICH BONHOEFFER

Let's get real. There is no hope for reconciliation and peace in relationships unless forgiveness lives. As you have read in this book, some of the heinous circumstances surrounding forgiveness make it brutally hard to contemplate. This kind of forgiveness is razor-sharp and edgy—it's not sappy or oversentimental.

Thank God that through the Holy Spirit the power to forgive is available to anyone, regardless of the rancor of the offense. But some X-factors additionally permeate the hope of forgiveness and restoration.

Prayer is one of the X-factors, the essential element that can jumpstart forgiveness and restoration. Prayer works in the unseen, the hearts of men and women, where it counts. The unseen is always God's most crucial and fruitful domain—it is the domain of the kingdom of heaven, that upside-down *terra incognita* (undocumented land). And if you are struggling to forgive someone, prayer is where you begin. In God's kingdom, the starting place is always to be still and quiet, pray, and not rush into action. God is never in a hurry.

Has someone refused to forgive you? Go deeper in prayer for them. You must choose to yield to the Spirit of prayer. It is where our lives intersect with the power of the Holy Spirit to accomplish God's purpose (unity). Regarding God healing our relationships, nothing is more important than prayer. If we are not praying, we rob ourselves of God's help.

Without prayer the enemy and his culture will lull us into going about our Christian life as if nothing is wrong, living with brokenness in relationship after relationship. Hidden offenses are buried deeply in our souls; honest communication is elusive, and the forces of darkness delight. Without prayer our lives proliferate with religious activity, much of it good—oh so very good! We work and work investing in insignificance, yet we have misinterpreted what is significant because of a lack of prayer.

Some practices in the Christian life indicate beauty and wholeness: serving others, hospitality, giving time and money, and so forth. When these qualities integrate into the fabric of our soul, we are primed to be godsends in the world. No single practice is more needed, significant, and influential than prayer. It needs to be the precursor to all these magnificent actions mentioned above. The brokenness in our world groans for the blessing that can be summoned by believing, persevering prayer.

There is much to be said about the necessity of prayer. Not the least of which is that God's very will and His glory are conditioned on prayer. But the truth is many of us live in a Christian culture that accepts and encourages comfort as a lifestyle, privacy as a premium, independence as an ideal, and sacrifice only when it is self-aggrandizing. Persistent prayer, what is that? On the whole, we tend to be a little lazy spiritually. Many Christians have grown indifferent to the veracity of prayer, which is courageous and will not be denied, but it persists importunately.

It may seem difficult to digest this thought, but persistent prayer moves God. Persistent prayer is what we need to infuse our spirit with God's Spirit. Jesus told us, "Ask, and it will be given to you; seek, and you will find; knock, and it will be opened to you" (Matt. 7:7, NASB). So what is Jesus saying in this passage? In Matthew 7:8-12 Jesus reveals that our prayers are based on the relationship of a father to his son. When his child asks for something, and the father knows it is suitable for him, the father eagerly provides it. However, a striking condition goes along with this promise of asking and receiving that we often overlook. The Father wants what is good for us. Prayer will never be a blank check; we fill in what we desire. Jesus is telling us in this Matthew passage He wants us to trust Him with our prayers and keep knocking.

Jesus instructs the disciples to pray in His name and trust Him. "If you ask anything in My name, I will do it" (John 14:14, NASB). The instruction about prayer is explicit, "pray in His name." Pray according to His will, what He knows is best for us. "This is the confidence which we have before Him, that, if we ask anything according to His will, He hears us" (1 John 5:14, NASB). When we pray in the name of Jesus, we are praying on the condition of His authority. We must submit to the King and His purposes to see the kingdom of heaven revealed in our relationships and lives.

This is the beauty of praying in Christ's name for healing in our relationships. It is explicitly within His will for us to live in oneness and unity with others. There is no question about this prayer. We cannot lose. Praying according to God's purposes energizes our will to take whatever necessary action to seek forgiveness and peace with others. Whether we are called to humble ourselves, assume responsibility for our actions, or do all we can do and then wait, we can become courageous.

We just keep knocking. We become undeterred. I'm still knocking. I have not succeeded entirely in this majestic journey toward forgiveness and restoration of relationships. We are not charged to do *more than* we can, but to do *everything* we can—back to one of our mantras, Romans 12:18 (NIV), "If it is possible, as far as it depends on you, live at peace with everyone." There are relationships in my life where I have gone the gamut—with as sincere a humility as I can muster through the Holy Spirit. But alas, a few Christian brothers and sisters have set the piers deeply. They will not budge. They will not consider forgiveness under any circumstance.

So what do I do? Like you, I keep knocking in prayer before the Lord in the quiet space. God has a timetable, and He has a lot of time.

When Herod Antipas imprisoned Peter, it came on the heels of Antipas having killed James, the first disciple martyred. Herod was emboldened and fully intended to have Peter killed too. Yet the very night when Peter was to be brought before Herod, an angel freed him. In the middle of the night, what were the disciples and others doing as the angel led Peter out of jail? You guessed it. They were praying!

> So Peter was kept in prison. But the church prayed to God without ceasing for him. The very night when Herod would have brought him out, Peter was sleeping between two soldiers, bound with two chains. And the guards before the door were securing the prison. And suddenly an angel of the Lord approached him, and a light shone in the prison. He struck Peter on the side and woke him up, saying, "Rise up, quickly." And the chains fell off his hands.
>
> —Acts 12:5-7

Only Luke's Gospel gives us these two magnificent stories pertinent to considering this X-factor of prayer in our relationships. Both stories speak pointedly to the necessity of persistence in prayer and never giving up when prayers are not answered.

> Then He said to them, "Which of you has a friend and shall go to him at midnight and say to him, 'Friend, lend me three loaves, for a friend of mine on his journey has come to me, and I have nothing to set before him'; and he will answer from within, 'Do not trouble me; the door is now shut, and my children are with me in bed; I cannot rise and give you anything'? I say to you, though he will not rise and give him anything because he is his friend, yet because of his persistence he will rise and give him as much as he needs."

—Luke 11:5-8

You may think this quest for forgiveness and restoration is pointless and the other parties involved care little. Trust God: His promises are true. Keep the faith. Keep knocking. The reality of prayer for most of us is that we have successes and failures. And we ponder why some of our prayers are answered and others are not.

> He told them a parable to illustrate that it is necessary always to pray and not lose heart. He said: "In a city there was a judge who did not fear God or regard man. And a widow was in that city. She came to him, saying, 'Avenge me against my adversary.' He would not for a while. Yet afterward he said to himself, 'Though I do not fear God or respect man, yet because this widow troubles me, I will avenge her, lest by her continual coming she will weary me.'"

—Luke 18:1-5

After Jesus tells the parable of the unjust judge, He speaks further:

And the Lord said, "Hear what the unjust judge says. And shall not God avenge His own elect and be patient with them, who cry *day and night* to Him? I tell you, He will avenge them speedily. Nevertheless, when the Son of Man comes, will He find faith on the earth?"

—Luke 18:6-8

Why are these two lessons so pivotal in our journey to resolve offense, bitterness, and separation? Because they speak so pointedly about the tenacity required in prayer. Notice those three words in italics, *day and night*. And let's hearken back to Peter, shackled in chains and guarded in prison. Many disciples of Jesus were praying fervently late into the night (Acts 12:5, 12).

Do you get the point?

You are not alone if you face seemingly impassable roadblocks in having someone forgive you. If you are contending for reconciliation, yet it seems further and further out of reach, remember our Savior. If your prayers appear to be unanswered, look closely at Jesus. On Maundy Thursday, Jesus was at the Mount of Olives praying to the Father to spare Him from suffering. And even earlier that day, Jesus had repeatedly prayed for the unity of His followers. Yet it remains a grim truth that Christ's prayers for the unity of His followers persist *unanswered*. The church is more divided today than at any time in history.

But we have this hope: Christ sits at the right hand of God almighty, maker of heaven and earth. Jesus intercedes for us according to God's will— unity with other Christians. Christ's intercession for us is perfect prayer. To our amazement, Jesus Christ invites regular, sinful, redeemed people like you and me to join Him as intercessors and to give our lives to prayer.

A Story of Redemption and Restored Relationships

Job's story is a stirring testimony to prayer's power in restoring lives and relationships.

Job was a wealthy man who was blameless and upright. Satan believed Job would curse God if he could get permission to punish Job and challenged God for the permission to do so. God, knowing Job's heart, allows Satan to torment Job to no end, but God forbids Satan from taking his life. As we know from the story, Job's testing is horrific. His loss is unfathomable. And in the end, he is left with horrible afflictions.

What did Job lose?

- Seven sons and three daughters.

- All his possessions: 7,000 sheep, 3,000 camels, 500 yokes of oxen, and very many servants—enough to care for all his animals, barns, fields, crops, etc.

- Job was struck with boils from the sole of his foot to the crown of his head. He sat in ashes and scraped his sores.

- Job went from the greatest of all the men of the East to nothing.

Three of Job's friends, Eliphaz, Bildad, and Zophar, come to visit him, and throughout the story these friends offer worthless advice and accuse Job that his suffering is a result of sin. In the crescendo ending, Job acknowledges God's unlimited power and admits the limitations of his human knowledge. God is pleased with Job's response but is upset with his worthless friends for their unsound advice. However, Job intercedes for them, and God forgives them. God restores all that Job had lost, and he ends up with twice as much as he started. Job lives a fruitful and long life.

But the Scripture states ever so profoundly, "The LORD also restored the fortunes of Job when he prayed for his friends, and the LORD increased double all that Job had" (Job 42:10, NASB). Job's prayers for his wayward friends saved them from their folly and activated God's restoration of his fortunes. The power of prayer is unlimited in renewing relationships when you put it into action.

Your relationships with family, friends, those you fellowship with, and in particular those you are separated from have never needed prayer more urgently and desperately than today. Jesus wants you to pray, and I pray this encouragement sinks deep into your soul.

The Pinnacle of Fellowship—the Eucharist, the Second X-Factor

We are no longer a hodgepodge group of sinners when we come to our Lord's Communion table. No, we become the bride, Jesus' body of followers that He invites to become one. The Lord's table is the quintessential expression of that oneness and unity. Every time we partake, we catch a foretaste of the ultimate restoration of all things and glimpse the marriage supper of the Lamb to come. Together, we celebrate the atoning work of Jesus Christ.

How important is the Lord's Supper? It is one of the two ordinances of the church, the other being baptism. Jesus instituted the sacrament of the Communion table to commemorate His death and denote the new covenant. Whether Protestant, Roman Catholic, or Orthodox, there is agreement that the Communion table symbolizes Christ's redemptive work: the fellowship of the people of God and the final marriage supper of the Lamb.

> Then I heard *something* like the voice of a great multitude and like the sound of many waters, and like the sound of mighty peals of thunder, saying, "Hallelujah! For the Lord our God, the Almighty, reigns. Let's rejoice and be glad and give the glory to Him, because the marriage of the Lamb has come, and His bride has prepared herself." It was given to her to clothe herself in fine linen, bright and clean; for the fine linen is the righteous acts of the saints. Then he said to me, "Write: 'Blessed are those who are invited to the wedding feast of the Lamb.'" And he said to me, "These are the true words of God."
>
> —Revelation 19:6-9, NASB

More Than Just the Eucharist

Dr. Robert Stamps, PhD, University of Nottingham, is one of the foremost theologians studying the Eucharist. Dr. Stamps' PhD dissertation was *The Doctrine of the Eucharist*. Brother Bob pointedly states that if Communion is relegated to just remembering Jesus, it becomes only a mental reflection of something that *was*. He says that Jesus' sacrifice can never be a *was*. Jesus is an *is*. He presents the Eucharist as being a "means" of grace. And Bob goes on to say that we have drifted away from what matters most with the Communion experience. We are changed when we partake of bread and the cup.[3]

Dr. Stamps' ideas support Paul's viewpoint as he writes about the Communion table in 1 Corinthians 11. The people were not treating Communion as the sacred sacrament it is. So Paul explained what he thought the Communion table should be.

> Therefore whoever eats this bread and drinks this cup of the Lord unworthily will be guilty of the body and blood of the Lord. Let a man examine himself and eat the bread and drink of the cup. For he who eats and drinks unworthily, eats and drinks damnation to himself, not discerning the Lord's body.
>
> —1 Corinthians 11:27-29

Read that last sentence again, slowly. Could there be any more serious consideration? Damnation to himself?

In the Sermon on the Mount, Jesus commands that if you bring your gift to the altar and remember that you are separated from another person, you should leave your gift and be reconciled to that person. Once this has happened, you should return and then offer your gift. "Therefore, if you bring your gift to the altar and there remember that your brother has something against you, leave your gift there before the altar and go on your way. First be reconciled to your brother, and then come and offer your gift" (Matt. 5:23-24).

The message concerning taking the Eucharist could not be more applicable to considering the importance of right relationships. We must take a "heart check" before taking Communion, including the penetrating question, "Am I divided from others or holding unforgiveness toward others?" When you come to the Lord's table, do you ask the Holy Spirit to reveal unrepentant sin against another or unforgiveness you are holding in your heart?

As difficult as it is to say, if we knowingly allow disunity to exist and come to the Lord's table, we are not worthy to partake. Jesus commands that all gossip, anger, envy, dissension, and unbrotherly conduct be resolved and must be resolved to partake of the Lord's Supper rightly.

When we come to the table together, do we experience the fellowship of the Spirit? For Dietrich Bonhoeffer, the table of our Lord was the archetypal event of unity. "The fellowship of the Lord's Supper is the superlative fulfillment of Christian fellowship. Here the community has reached its goal. The life of Christians together under the Word has reached its perfection in the sacrament."[4]

Not seeking to live in forgiveness with others will breed disunity in the body of Christ. Few things are more destructive to Christ's intentions on earth, but nothing gives the enemy greater delight.

Let us resolve to give the Lamb the reward of His suffering—unity with the brethren.

For this reason I bow my knees to the Father of our Lord Jesus Christ, from whom the whole family in heaven and earth is named, that He would give you, according to the riches of His glory, power to be strengthened by His Spirit in the inner man, and that Christ may dwell in your hearts through faith; that you, being rooted and grounded in love, may be able to comprehend with all saints what is the breadth and length and depth and height, and to know the love of Christ which surpasses knowledge; that you may be filled with all the fullness of God.

Now to Him who is able to do exceedingly abundantly beyond all that we ask or imagine, according to the power that works in us, to Him be the glory in the church and in Christ Jesus throughout all generations, forever and ever. Amen.

—Ephesians 3:14-21

CHAPTER 13

PARTING WAYS: A POSTSCRIPT

They had such a sharp disagreement that they parted company. Barnabas took Mark and sailed for Cyprus, but Paul chose Silas and left.

—Acts 15:39-40a, NIV

Here are two of the stalwarts of the early Christian faith. Paul, the great apostle, wrote thirteen or fourteen of the twenty-seven books in the New Testament. He spent twenty years making three missionary incursions throughout the Roman Empire (from Asia Minor to Europe), spreading the gospel and planting churches. Paul was the prophet who brought the gospel to non-Jews. His impact on the kingdom of God is immeasurable. Tradition holds that he was beheaded in Rome and died a martyr at the order of Nero.

And Barnabas? He was no lightweight. Barnabas was an early Christian follower and became prominent in the Jerusalem church. He was all in with the church, selling his land and giving the proceeds to the community.

Christian tradition suggests that Barnabas was stoned to death for his preaching of the gospel.

Paul and Barnabas were close. After Paul's conversion and upon returning to Jerusalem, Barnabas was the one who went out on a limb to introduce Paul, this former persecutor of the Christians, to the apostles. Later in Acts 11:25-26, Barnabas sought Paul out to have him help teach the new believers in Antioch. They even traveled together on the first incredible missionary journey for two years and approximately fourteen hundred miles! Yet it happened: after years of friendship and ministry together, a disagreement, a sharp dispute so profound they parted company. In Greek, the word *sharp* (Acts 15:39) connotes violent anger and passion.[1] This was no minor misunderstanding.

Some surprisingly cogent lessons can be drawn from Paul and Barnabas' conflict and separation. These lessons are applicable and crucial for us two thousand years later.

Earnest followers of Jesus can have sharp disagreements and conflicts.

Paul and Barnabas; their names went together like Peter and John. Through all the years and experiences, they weathered the storms of ministry and life together. Yet they had a severe conflict over John Mark. Christians can disagree passionately.

The Scriptures don't reveal if one apostle was right and the other was wrong. We don't know if there was a failure with one of the men. There may have been a failure with both. But if men of this spiritual stature can have intense conflict, why would we think we are immune from such experiences with other Christians, mature Christians? You and I are just like Paul and Barnabas—imperfect. James puts it this way, "For we all stumble in many ways" (Jas. 3:2a, NASB).

Earnest followers of Jesus can disagree and go their separate ways.

Relationships end for numerous reasons. People move, change occupations, or seek further education and training. Friends believe the Lord is taking their lives in different directions as their priorities change. Close relationships can end because of misunderstandings and conflict.

Sometimes we will honestly disagree and part ways with other believers. Sometimes things can't be worked out between people, no matter how hard we try. But that doesn't mean we can't still love and honor one another, as Paul and Barnabas did. It matters how they ended. It matters how you end relationships.

We must always leave the door open for the restoration of relationships.

Paul, Barnabas, and John Mark respected each other, recognized each other's importance and contribution to the furtherance of the gospel, and more than likely had constructive interactions following their initial separation. Paul later positively mentioned Barnabas and John Mark in his letters (1 Cor. 9:6; 2 Tim. 4:11).

"Or is it only Barnabas and I who have no right to refrain from working? Who goes to war at any time at his own expense? Who plants a vineyard, but does not eat of its fruit? Or who feeds a flock, but does not drink of the flock's milk?" (1 Cor. 9:6-7).

"Only Luke is with me. Get Mark, and bring him with you, for he is profitable to me for the ministry" (2 Tim. 4:11).

Joseph Benson, in his commentary on 1 Corinthians 9:6, makes this observation, "The honorable mention which Paul makes of Barnabas in this passage deserves notice, as it shows that these good men, notwithstanding their sharp contention about John Mark, Acts 15:13, entertained no resentment against each other on that account, but mutually esteemed each other: and perhaps, on some occasions after that, preached the gospel together, as before."[2]

Here is the great lesson we all must contemplate deeply and honestly before the Lord when it comes to parting ways, for whatever reason. You can tell everything about a person by how they end a relationship. And if the impetus for bringing the relationship to closure is primarily with one person, you can tell everything about the other person by how they respond. The challenge is to be Christlike in all we do.

Let me suggest a short biblical model to follow in bringing relationships to an end if people are interested in demonstrating Christlike attitudes and actions. Three principles are absolute confidentiality, choosing to bless, and leaving the door open to the opportunity for forgiveness and restoration.

When it comes to confidentiality, we are all tested. And the confidentiality test is one God wants us to pass with an A+. We dishonor the Lord when we fail this test and share, unnecessarily, with others the details of why or how we parted ways with other believers. When we don't practice confidentiality, we become the gossip and separate people. We cause people to choose sides.

In ending relationships, Christians should prioritize blessing one another and affirm that the Lord wants us to walk in forgiveness toward one another. Bring all the issues to a proper end, as much as possible, and end the parting with prayer. Ending relationships can be one of the most challenging interactions we face with people. We must call on the Lord's grace, mercy, and forgiveness. And He has plenty of it for us. "And God is able to make all grace overflow to you, so that, always having all sufficiency in everything, you may abundance for every good deed" (2 Cor. 9:8, NASB).

A relationship where people choose not to bless each other may take years to heal. If we refuse to bless the other party when we go our separate ways, we will unknowingly create a blockage in our hearts. The Scriptures instruct us to guard our hearts. It is crucial for the full functioning of the power of the Holy Spirit in our lives to have hearts free of offense, unforgiveness, and ill feelings toward anyone.

I have witnessed and experienced the restoration of fellowship decades after it ended due to conflict. It is sweet; it is precious. It is a testimony to non-believers. Psalm 133:1-2 (NLT) expresses the heart of God over Christians who can live harmoniously: "How wonderful and pleasant it is when brothers live together in harmony! For harmony is as precious as the anointing oil that was poured over Aaron's head, that ran down his beard and onto the border of his robe."

A relationship may end over disagreements, even intense conflict, but we must be open to whatever God may do with the relationship at a future time. Harmony and restoration are like the ointment of Psalm 133:1-2. Benson's commentary speaks of it in these terms:

> It (harmony) is like the precious ointment—It is no less grateful and refreshing than that holy anointing oil, which was strongly perfumed, and diffused its fragrance all around, to the great delight of all present. This verse is explained by Exodus 13:23 where God gave directions concerning the ointment which was to anoint Aaron and his sons. It was to be composed of several rich spices, which, by being rightly tempered and mixed together, yielded a most fragrant odor and thus became a most expressive emblem of unanimity and concord, in a well-cemented society; all jointly conspiring and contributing, according to their various capacities, tempers, and conditions, to the good of the whole.[1]

Wow! Can you remember your sweetest time of fellowship with other believers? This fellowship is meant to be an aroma, an atmosphere that entices and draws unbelievers to the kingdom of heaven on earth.

Do we bless or curse? Are we any different from the world? When the world witnesses Christians fight, gossip, and end relationships with bitterness and unforgiveness, it confirms their disbelief. Christianity is not real. Christianity does not work.

What if our goal in ending a relationship was ministering kindness and gentleness? God's kingdom on earth would be glorified if nothing else were achieved!

The world is always watching to see how Christians end relationships.

Notes

Introduction

1. C. S. Lewis, *The Voyage of the Dawn Treader* (New York: HarperCollins, 2002), 227.

2. Lacy Clark Ellman, "Thin Spaces, Holy Spaces: Where Do You Encounter God," A Sacred Journey, https://www.asacredjourney.net/thin-places/ (accessed February 21, 2021).

3. St. Patrick of Ireland, "St Patrick's Breastplate," Goodreads, https://www.goodreads.com/quotes/413139-christ-with-me-christ-before-me-christ-behind-me-christ (accessed February 27, 2021).

Chapter 1: My Confession

1. A. J. Russell, *God Calling Journal* (Uhrichsville, Ohio: Barbour Publishing Inc., 1953), 332.

2. Author unknown, "A Confederate Soldier's Prayer," Virginia Public Radio, Civil War Series, https://www.wvtf.org/civil-war-series/2019-12-15/an-un-known-confederate-soldier (accessed March 29, 2021).

3. J. I. Packer, Joel Scandrett, "17 Questions about Salvation," Crossway, https://www.crossway.org/articles/17-questions-about-salvation/ (accessed April, 27, 2021).

Chapter 2: The Greatest Miracle

1. M. Basilea Schlink, *Repentance: The Joy-Filled Life* (Germany: Evangelical Sisterhood of Mary, 2016), 9.

2. Bible Hub, *Strong's Concordance*. Copyright © 2021 by Discovery Bible. s.v. "semeion," OT4592. https://biblehub.com/greek/4592.htm (accessed March 21, 2021).

3. Inbar Maayan, "The Miracle of Life (1983), by NOVA," Embryo Project Encyclopedia, November 19, 2010, https://embryo.asu.edu/pages/miracle-life-1983-nova (accessed April 30, 2021).

4. St. Augustine of Hippo, "The House of My Soul Is Narrow," Catholic News Agency, https://www.catholicnewsagency.com/resource/56328/the-house-of-my-soul-is-narrow-%E2%80%93-st-augustine-of-hippo (accessed May 31, 2021).

Chapter 3: Forgiveness: The Oil of the Spirit

1. Ronald Bingham, *The Making of the Beautiful: The Story of Annie Johnson Flint* (Columbia, SC: Hayden Press Publishing, 2019), 56.

2. St. Ignatius of Loyola, "The Prayer for Generosity," myUSF, https://myusf.usfca.edu/jesuit/poems-prayers-short-meditations (accessed June 4, 2021).

3. C. S. Lewis, *The Screwtape Letters* (Broadway, NY: HarperCollins Publishers, 2001), 5.

4. Gerald Hopkins, "As Kingfishers Catch Fire," The Poetry Foundation, https://www.poetryfoundation.org/poems/44389/as-kingfishers-catch-fire (accessed June 22, 2021).

5. N. T. Wright. *Matthew for Everyone*, Part 2 (London, UK: Westminster John Knox Press; 3rd Edition, 2004), 182.

6. Joyce Meyers, QuoteFancy, https://quotefancy.com/quote/846156/Joyce-Meyer-Forgiveness-is-not-a-feeling-it-s-a-decision-we-make-because-we-want-to-do (accessed August 2, 2021).

7. Bible Hub, *NAS Exhaustive Concordance of the Bible with Hebrew-Aramaic and Greek Dictionaries.* Copyright © 1981, 1998 by The Lockman Foundation, *"hos,"* NT5613. https://biblehub.com/text/matthew/6-12.htm (accessed October 4, 2021).

8. Marianne Williamson, BrainyQuote, https://www.brainyquote.com/quotes/marianne_williamson_635346 (accessed January 12, 2022).

9. Bible Hub, *NAS Exhaustive Concordance of the Bible with Hebrew-Aramaic and Greek Dictionaries.*

10. Dr. Jud David, "God 10,000 Talents and Forgiving a Sinning Brother," Lion and the Lamb, *The Herald-News*, https://www.rheaheraldnews.com/lifestyles/article_334f283e-8262-11e5-aaf7-53cf9a2b76bb.html#:~:text=In%20

Matthew%2018%3A23%2C%20Jesus,owes%20him%20100%20day's%20 wages (accessed April 13, 2022).

11. Google.com dictionary, s.v. "eternity," https://www.google.com/ search?q=eternity&oq=eternity&aqs=chrome..69i57j0i433i512j46i175i199i-512j0i512j0i433i512l2j46i175i199i512j0i512j46i512j0i433i512.2893j0j15&-sourceid=chrome&ie=UTF-8 (accessed May 4, 2022).

12. Warren W. Wiersbe, *The Wiersbe Bible Commentary: New Testament* (Colorado Springs, CO: David C. Cook, 2007), Mark 2:1-22, 93-96.

Chapter 4: Bad Theology

1. C. S. Lewis, *Mere Christianity* (New York: Touchstone, 1996), 176.

2. Google.com dictionary, s.v. "theology," https://www.google.com/ search?q=what+does+the+word+theology+mean&oq=&aqs=-chrome.3.35i39i362l8.4667520j0j15&sourceid=chrome&ie=UTF-8 (accessed July 12, 2022).

3. Young Praise, "The wise man built his house upon the rock (with lyrics)," YouTube, February 26, 2011, https://www.youtube.com/watch?v=d-kNOcr5iHP4 (accessed August 24, 2022).

4. Bible Hub, *Brown-Driver-Briggs Hebrew and English Lexicon*, unabridged, electronic database. Copyright © 2002, 2003, 2006 by Biblesoft Inc., "yare," OT 3372. https://biblehub.com/hebrew/3372.htm (accessed September 2, 2022).

5. Bible Hub, *Brown-Driver-Briggs Hebrew and English Lexicon*. https://biblehub.com/hebrew/3374.htm (accessed September 2, 2022).

6. Howard Simon, "I Choose the Mountain," PoemHunter.com, https://www.poemhunter.com/poem/i-choose-the-mountain/ (accessed September 30, 2022).

Chapter 5: Now Open Your Bosom to the Wind's Free Play

1. Bible Hub, *Englishman's Concordance*, electronic database. Copyright © 2002, 2003, 2006 by Biblesoft Inc., s.v. *"ehad,"* OT 259. https://biblehub.com/hebrew/echad_259.htm (accessed October 20, 2022).

2. Jools, "Review: 'No Longer Strangers' By Greg Cole," The Freedom Trust, October 27, 2021, https://truefreedomtrust.co.uk/review-no-longer-strangers-greg-coles (accessed November 1, 2022).

3. Bible Hub, *Strong's Concordance*, s.v. *"pleroo"*, NT 4137. https://biblehub.com/greek/4137.htm (November 14, 2022).

4. George MacDonald, "The Diary of an Old Soul, May 21," https://diaryofanoldsoul.com/poems/142 (accessed November 30, 2022).

5. Johanna Augusta, quoted in Laruen David, "The Spiritual Meaning of Doves + What to Do If They Keep Appearing," mbg mindfulness, December 16, 2022, https://www.mindbodygreen.com/articles/dove-symbolism (accessed December 21, 2022).

6. Tick, "The Dove: The Gentle, Empathetic-Optimistic Personality," https://tick.com.au/tick-dove-personality-type/#:~:text=While%20shy%20and%20friendly%2C%20doves,their%20heels%20into%20the%20sand (accessed January 2, 2023).

7. *Merriam-Webster*, s.v. "sensitive," https://www.merriam-webster.com/dictionary/sensitive (accessed January 2, 2023).

8. *Merriam-Webster*, s.v. "innocence," https://www.merriam-webster.com/dictionary/innocence (accessed January 3, 2023).

9. Tobin Duby, "Counterfeit Bills," Classical Conversations, April 5, 2012, https://members.classicalconversations.colm/article/counterfeit-bills (accessed January 15, 2023).

10. The New International Version, Ephesians 4, BibleGateway, https://www.biblegateway.com/passage/?search=ephesians+4&version=NIV (accessed January 27, 2023).

11. R. C. Sproul, *The Mystery of the Holy Spirit* (Scotland, UK: Christian Focus Publications, 1990), 8.

Chapter 6: Why So Little of the Kingdom of Heaven?

1. George E. Ladd, *The Gospel of the Kingdom* (Grand Rapids, MI: Wm. B. Eerdmans Publishing Co, 1959), 15.

2. Richard J. Foster, *Celebration of Discipline* (San Francisco: HarperOne, 2018), Contents.

3. Edward Elliott, *The Best of Andrew Murray on Prayer* (Uhrichsville, OH: Barbour Publishing, 1952), October 26.

4. L. B. Cowman, *Streams in the Desert* (Grand Rapids, MI: Zondervan, 1966), 251.

5. C. S. Lewis, *The Screwtape Letters* (New York: Touchstone, 1996), 130.

6. Thomas Merton, Goodreads, https://www.goodreads.com/quotes/8676525-but-give-me-the-strength-that-waits-upon-you-in (accessed February 4, 2023).

7. Wikipedia, "Canyon, Capertee Valley," https://www.google.com/search?sxsrf=ALiCzsZCHGofKJx4QHhlBc5smlqICHeC4w:1668619387653&q=what+is+the+widest+canyon+in+the+world&spell=1&sa=X&ved=2ahUKEwj8z_bOm7P7AhVPjYkEHTlMCckQBSgAegQIBhAB&biw=1280&bih=689&dpr=2 (accessed February 7, 2023).

8. T. Austin-Sparks, Austin-Sparts.net, https://www.austin-sparks.net/english/books/000987.html (accessed February 19, 2023).

9. E. Stanley Jones, *Christian Maturity* (Nashville, TN: Abingdon Press, 1957), 74.

Chapter 7: Offense—Enough Said

1. Frances J. Roberts, *Come Away My Beloved* (Northridge, CA: Voice Publications, 1968), 53.

2. Bible Hub, *Matthew Henry's Concise Commentary*, Matthew 18:7-14, https://biblehub.com/commentaries/matthew/18-7.htm (accessed March 2, 2023).

3. Dr. Jeffery Beyer, coffee shop conversations, circa March 2023.

4. *Guidepost*, "Guidepost's Classics: Corrie ten Boom on Forgiveness," https://guideposts.org/positive-living/guideposts-classics-corrie-ten-boom-forgiveness/ (accessed March 29, 2023).

5. Dave Kopel, Maria Goretti Network/MGN Recovery Through Forgiveness, "St. Maria Goretti Story," https://mgoretti.org/mgstory (accessed March 29, 2023).

6. Joesph Shapiro, NPR, "Amish Forgive School Shooter, Struggle with Grief," October 2, 2007, https://www.npr.org/2007/10/02/14900930/amish-forgive-school-shooter-struggle-with-grief (accessed March 30, 2023).

7. Abraham Joshua Heschel, *The Sabbath* (New York: Farrar, Straus and Giroux, 1951), 3.

8. Christine Westoff, *Reframing the Prophetic Study Guide*, chapter 9, pg. 6.

9. *Merriam-Webster*, s.v. "enemy," https://www.merriam-webster.com/dictionary/enemy (accessed January 3, 2023).

10. Pastor Stratman, "A Collection of Prayers: Christian Prayers, Ancient and Modern," The Holy Spirit, 1st stanza, St. Augustine of Hippo, https://acollectionofprayers.com/2018/05/20/the-holy-spirit/ (accessed March 13, 2023).

Chapter 8: Don't Shut the Door with Your Words

1. Harry Verploegh, *Oswald Chambers: The Best from All His Books* (Nashville, TN: Oliver-Nelson Books, 1987), 380.

2. Ligonier Ministries, "The Purpose of Wisdom Literature," January 1, 2015, https://www.ligonier.org/learn/devotionals/purpose-wisdom-literature#:~:-text=We%20read%20in%20Proverbs%201,the%20Wisdom%20Books%20is%20not (accessed March 24, 2023).

3. C. S. Lewis, *Mere Christianity* (New York: HarperCollins Publishers, 2001), 208.

4. The Dialog, "Woe to those who gossip, as Pope Francis has consistently warned," by Elise Italiano Ureneck, https://thedialog.org/opinion/woe-to-those-who-gossip-as-pope-francis-has-consistently-warned/ (accessed May 18, 2023).

Chapter 9: Breaking the Sword

1. Oswald Chambers, *My Utmost For His Highest Journal* (Uhrichsville, OH: Barbour Publishing, 1963), November 23.

Chapter 10: Mission Possible: Forgiveness and Reconciliation in Families

1. Wisconsin Public Radio, "After years in conflict zones, a war reporter reckons with a deadly cancer diagnosis," by Terry Gross, https://www.wpr.org/news/after-years-in-conflict-zones-a-war-reporter-reckons-with-a-deadly-cancer-

diagnosis#:~:text=Rod%20Nordland%20looks%20at%20the,terminal%20
brain%20cancer%2C%20in%202019 (accessed March 4, 2024).

2. Alan Kreider, *The Patient Ferment of the Early Church: The Improbable Rise of Christianity in the Roman Empire* (Grand Rapids, MI: Baker Publishing Group, 2016), 2.

3. Kevin Carson, "Wisdom for Life in Christ Together," https://kevincarson.com/2019/07/25/if-it-werent-for-christians-id-be-a-christian-gandhi/ (accessed, July 21, 2023).

4. Generosity Monk, "Columba: Last Words of Blessing," https://generositymonk.com/2021/08/19/columba-last-words-of-blessing/ (accessed August 4, 2023).

Chapter 11: The Twin Demons of Destruction: Gossip and Betrayal

1. Reuters, "Pope Says Gossiping Is a 'Worse Plague' Than Coronavirus," https://www.reuters.com/article/us-pope-gossip/pope-says-gossiping-is-a-worse-plague-than-coronavirus-idUSKBN25X0K9 (accessed September 18, 2023).

2. Ian Morgan Cron and Suzanne Stabile, *The Road Back to You* (Downers Grove, IL: IVP Books, 2016), 61.

3. *The Guardian*, "Pope Francis Says Gossip Is 'a Plague Worse Than Covid,'" https://www.theguardian.com/world/2020/sep/06/pope-francis-says-gossip-is-a-plague-worse-than-covid (accessed September 22, 2023).

4. Billy Graham Evangelistic Association of Canada, Answers, https://www.billygraham.ca/answer/i-wish-youd-say-something-about-gossiping-because-i-dont-think-people-realize-just-how-destructive-it-can-be-am-i-right-or-am-i-just-too-sensitive-to-what-people-say-about-me/ (accessed September 31, 2023).

5. Gene Edwards, *The Prisoner in the Third Cell* (Auburn, ME: The Seedsowers), 0.

6. Nightbirde, "God Is on the Bathroom Floor," https://www.nightbirde.co/blog/2021/9/27/god-is-on-the-bathroom-floor (accessed October 19. 2023).

7. M. Basilea Schlink, *Repentance*, 39.

Chapter 12: The X-Factors

1. Dietrich Bonhoeffer, *Life Together* (New York: Harper & Row Publishers), 86.

2. Definitions from Oxford Languages (accessed January 16, 2024).

3. Dr. Robert J. Stamps, YouTube, "The Meaning of Communion: Robert Stamps," https://www.youtube.com/watch?v=UJDdFdFrBtU (accessed January 29, 2024).

4. Dietrich Bonhoeffer, *Life Together*, 122.

Chapter 13: Parting Ways: A Postscript

1. Bible Hub, *Thayer's Greek Lexicon Strongs NT* 3948, Acts 15: 39, https://biblehub.com/greek/3948.htm (accessed May 19, 2024).

2. Bible Hub, Benson Commentary, 1 Cor. 9:6,

3. https://biblehub.com/commentaries/1_corinthians/9-6.htm (accessed May 25, 2024).

Author Contact

If you would like to contact Tim, find out more information, purchase books, or request him to speak, please contact:

Tim Cameron

4665 S. Trenton Ave.

Tulsa, Oklahoma

74105

Cell: 918.237.5891

Email: timcameron8245@gmail.com

NOTES

NOTES

NOTES

www.ingramcontent.com/pod-product-compliance
Lightning Source LLC
Chambersburg PA
CBHW030828090426
42737CB00009B/919